Dear Missionaries Volume 2

Letters to Member Missionaries of the Church of Jesus Christ of Latter-day Saints (The Mormons)

Ritchey M. Marbury III

RIMAR BOOKS

Copyright © 2017 by Ritchey M. Marbury III
RIMAR BOOKS
All rights reserved; however,
If good is found here, feel free to share it
ISBN-10: 0692833331
ISBN-13: 9780692833339
All images by Ritchey M. Marbury III

Dedication

This book is dedicated to a man born on my birthday—except he was born twenty years earlier. I was born May 18, 1938. He was born May 18, 1918. Years before I joined the Church of Jesus Christ of Latter-day Saints, he shared books with me, visited me, and sent missionaries to teach me. He was the mission president of the Florida Mission during many of the years I studied the Church. Today, some forty-seven years after my baptism, he remains my friend. Even at the age of ninety-eight, which is his age at the time of this writing, his mind is alert and his wit keen.

This man is Glen L. Rudd. I love and respect him as an eternal friend and mentor. I am a better man for knowing him, as are all others who are fortunate enough to know him. If greatness is measured by service to others, Glen Rudd is one of the greatest.

Today, December 31, 2016, just before sending this book to be reviewed and proofread by the publisher, I received a phone call telling me that Glen Rudd died a few hours ago. This world is a better place because of his influence. I miss him already, but I know I shall see him again and we will continue to be friends throughout all eternity.

Contents

Introduction	ix
A Few Short Years	1
A Psalm Of Life	5
Albatross	7
Ask	10
Assistant's Presentation	13
Be One	16
Be Wise	19
Ben Franklin's New Year Advice	21
Captain's Daughter	23
Character Lessons	25
College For Dessert	27
Confession	29
Criticism Or Example	31
David Tarried Still At Jerusalem	33
Devastation And Recovery	35
Dick Beason's New Year's Resolutions	39
Donuts And Temptation	43
Dreams And Prayers	45
Easter Lily	47
Every Member A Missionary	50
Examine Yourself	53
Faith Is Like A Muscle	55
Faith Works	57
Faster Than A Speeding Horse	59
Folded Napkin	62
Forever Family	64
Forgotten	67
Glen L. Rudd Teaches	69

God Is Not Mocked	73
Happiness Is Like Pages In Your Journal	75
Harold B. Lee's Example	78
Hold Fast	80
House By The Side Of The Road	84
How Did You Die?	87
How To Improve Ability To Teach	89
Humility Is A Virtue	92
I Can	94
I Went To See My Dentist	96
In God We Trust	98
It Can Be Done	100
Jest 'Fore Christmas	102
Joseph Smith Testifies Of Jesus Christ	106
Just Call Me	109
Keep A-Goin'	111
Keep Pecking Away	113
Last House On The Street	115
Leaky Roof	117
Lessons From My Father	120
Lessons From My Mother	122
Life Is Forever	124
Live Or Die, It's A Win-Win	127
Make Someone Happy	129
Manner Of Happiness	131
Matthew Cowley's Good Night's Sleep	133
Mighty Change Of Heart	136
Mother's Day Tribute	138
My Choice	141
My Soul Delighteth In Plainness	143
Nadine Oldham	145
Nobility	148
Not In Vain	151
Nothing Shall Be Impossible	153
Old Home Place	158
Only A Dad	160
Only Doers Fail	162

Pounding On Bent Nails	164
Prayer Feeds Missionary	166
Preparation Precedes Performance	168
Prepare Or Procrastinate	171
Red Knot Success Habits	174
Reject Debt	177
Repent And Find Inner Peace	181
Search The Scriptures	183
See The Good In Cordele	185
Seek First The Kingdom Of God	188
Sermons We See	190
Six Days Shalt Thou Work	193
Smart What?	196
Spiritually Correct	198
Sweet Kiss Of Death	200
Ten Commandments Today	202
Thanks For Gnats	204
Things Jesus Taught	206
Thoughts On Life	209
To Thine Own Self Be True	212
Together In Life And Eternity	214
Tribute To Mother	218
Ugly Purple Scarf	220
Venus Flytrap—Nature's Deadly Tantalizer	222
Wanting To Or Willing To	225
What Is The Price?	227
What Is The Risk?	229
Why Me?	232
Will	245
Wisdom From Prophets	247
Wishbone Or Backbone	251
Words Of Wisdom From The Past	253
Words Without Knowledge	256
Ideas For Missionary Service	258
About The Author	263

INTRODUCTION

Dear Missionaries,

   What is the significance of the folded napkin left at the tomb of the resurrected Savior? What does the speed of a horse have to do with the restored gospel? What council did Benjamin Franklin give regarding the New Year? How did Dick Beason's page-a-day plan uncover the cause of the fall of the Nephite culture? Why should we be thankful for gnats?
   These letters provide the answers and relate spiritual and motivational messages to all members of the Church of Jesus Christ of Latter-day Saints. Many years ago, a prophet of God, David O. McKay, spoke these words: "Every member a missionary." Since we are all missionaries, this book of letters entitled *Dear Missionaries: Volume 2* applies to all of us.
   God has not ceased to perform miracles, and I include many in these letters. They tell of an infant girl run over by a car, the blessing her father gave her, and how my wife, Fonda, and I saw her alive and healthy the next Sunday at church. They tell of a man dying of cancer, his blessing by missionaries, and his cure. They tell of prayers for a missionary answered immediately by someone more than one thousand miles away.
   These letters tell faith-promoting experiences and motivational stories, and they teach principles that enrich lives and encourage you to act upon the faith you already have. If your faith is weak, these letters will strengthen that faith. Some of the letters are included simply for your enjoyment. After all, the scriptures teach us that one of the purposes of life is to have joy.
   I write these letters to all who read this book. I will not know many of you, but I trust you will grow closer to Heavenly Father

and Jesus Christ as you read them. Part of the motivation for writing this book was due to Glen L. Rudd. He served as mission president while Fonda and I investigated the Church. He later became a general authority. He was kind enough to give us copies of books containing his treasured experiences and other notes. Reading his books provided much of the motivation necessary to write these letters. To quote from his words on the last page of his *Scrap & Note Book II*, "In every happening there is a story: Find it. Write it down. Use it."

Although many of the letters include actual names and places, I omitted many names due to the spiritual nature of the experiences. Some reading this book will recognize the experiences to be their own. If they wish, those persons involved may choose to provide their names and give a more detailed account of the experiences described.

Enjoy and grow stronger in your faith and love of the Savior—as I have.

Love,

Ritchey Marbury

"One of the greatest discoveries in life is finding a dependable person."

—Richard L. Evans

Joseph and Hyrum Smith

A Few Short Years

Dear Missionaries,

Jesus Christ lived a few short years—thirty-three. He spent only three in public ministry. We know little of His boyhood. The secular scholars of His time wrote little about Him. The New Testament of the Bible describes the most detailed history of His life, yet tells only a fragment of His teachings and accomplishments. Indeed, John 21:25 tells us, "And there are also many other things which Jesus did, the which, if they should be written every one, I suppose that even the world itself could not contain the books that should be written."

In a few short years, Jesus did more to inspire the world to do good than any other being that ever lived. He made it possible for all to have everlasting life and to return to live forever with that God in Heaven who gave us life. He taught us that the most important commandment is to "love the Lord thy God with all thy heart, and with all thy soul, and with all thy mind" (Matthew 22:37). He taught that the second commandment is "Thou shalt love thy neighbor as thyself" (Matthew 22:39).

Jesus lived a perfect life. He went with his parents to the temple at the age of twelve. When they could not find Him on their journey home, they returned to the temple. There they found Him. When asked why He was not with them, Jesus replied, "Wist ye not that I must be about my Father's business?" (Luke 2:49).

Luke 2:52 teaches, "Jesus increased in wisdom and stature, and in favor with God and man." This reminds us that we should strive to grow mentally, physically, spiritually, and socially.

Jesus overcame temptations. When tempted by the devil, He responded with faith in His Heavenly Father and knowledge of the scriptures. After fasting forty days and nights, the devil presented diverse temptations. Jesus answered by quoting scriptures.

"It is written, Man shall not live by bread alone, but by every word that proceedeth out of the mouth of God" (Matthew 4:4). "It is written again, Thou shalt not tempt the Lord thy God" (Matthew 4:7). "Get thee hence, Satan, for it is written, Thou shalt worship the Lord thy God, and him only shalt thou serve" (Matthew 4:10).

Jesus taught us to love one another, to forgive one another, and to go about doing good. He taught us to be totally obedient to our Father in Heaven. Jesus taught by example. He healed the sick and made the blind to see and the lame to walk.

At the Garden of Gethsemane, He took upon Himself the sins of the world. Luke 22:42 records He prayed saying, "Father, if thou be willing, remove this cup from me: nevertheless not my will, but thine be done." Luke continues to record Christ's agony. "And being in agony he prayed more earnestly: and his sweat was as it were great drops of blood falling down to the ground" (Luke 22:44).

While dying on the cross, He prayed to Heavenly Father to forgive those at His crucifixion, for they knew not what they were doing. Later he cried with a loud voice, "Father, into thy hands I commend my spirit" (Luke 23:46). Then He willingly gave up the ghost.

The first day of the week after Christ's crucifixion, Mary Magdalene and other faithful women went to Christ's tomb bringing spices and other ointments they had prepared for the anointing of His body. They entered the tomb, but Jesus was not there. Two angels appeared and asked, "Why seek ye the living among the dead?" The angels spoke again, "He is not here, but is risen" (Luke 24:5–6).

Many saw the resurrected Christ. Mary Magdalene, a woman, was the first. He talked to other women somewhere between the sepulcher and Jerusalem. He spoke to two disciples on the road to Emmaus and to Peter in or near Jerusalem, and to ten of the apostles and others at Jerusalem. He spoke to eleven of the apostles at the Sea of Tiberias, on a mountain in Galilee, and at the time of His ascension at the Mount of Olives near Bethany.

The Bible records in 1 Corinthians 15:5–7 that Cephas, who was then one of the twelve, saw Jesus. Later, more than five hundred brethren saw Him. Then James saw Him. Paul also records in 1 Corinthians 15: 8 that he saw Him.

The Book of Mormon, Another Testament of Jesus Christ, tells of the resurrected Christ's visit to the Western Hemisphere. Many saw Him, heard Him teach, and witnessed how He blessed little children.

Jesus Christ is the only begotten Son of our Heavenly Father. He lived and died a voluntary death as a consecrated sacrifice for the sins of all persons who live, have lived, or yet shall live. His literal resurrection from death to immortality gives us hope and assurance that there is life after death. Death is a temporary separation of the body from the spirit. It is not permanent. We will live again because of the sacrifice of our Savior, Jesus Christ.

Love,

Ritchey Marbury

"For since by man came death, by man came also the resurrection of the dead. For as in Adam all die, even so in Christ shall all be made alive."

—1 CORINTHIANS 15:21–22

A Psalm Of Life

Dear Missionaries,

In his poem, "A Psalm of Life," Henry Wadsworth Longfellow taught a great lesson in how to live. Ponder its message as you read it.

> Tell me not, in mournful numbers,
> Life is but an empty dream!—
> For the soul is dead that slumbers,
> And things are not what they seem.
>
> Life is real! Life is earnest!
> And the grave is not its goal;
> Dust thou art, to dust returnest,
> Was not spoken of the soul.
>
> Not enjoyment, and not sorrow,
> Is our destined end or way;
> But to act, that each to-morrow
> Find us farther than to-day.
>
> Art is long, and Time is fleeting,
> And our hearts, though stout and brave,
> Still, like muffled drums, are beating
> Funeral marches to the grave.

In the world's broad field of battle,
In the bivouac of Life,
Be not like dumb, driven cattle!
Be a hero in the strife!

Trust no Future, howe'er pleasant!
Let the dead Past bury its dead!
Act,—act in the living Present!
Heart within, and God o'erhead!

Lives of great men all remind us
We can make our lives sublime,
And, departing, leave behind us
Footprints on the sands of time;

Footprints, that perhaps another,
Sailing o'er life's solemn main,
A forlorn and shipwrecked brother,
Seeing, shall take heart again.

Let us, then, be up and doing,
With a heart for any fate;
Still achieving, still pursuing,
Learn to labor and to wait.

Love,

Ritchey Marbury

"Life is real! Life is earnest!
And the grave is not its goal;
Dust thou art, to dust returnest,
Was not spoken of the soul."

—HENRY WADSWORTH LONGFELLOW

ALBATROSS

Dear Missionaries,

Greed destroys. It destroys the well-being of the victim and eventually the well-being of the greedy. Consider the albatross.

The albatross is a bird of the open seas and a master of dynamic soaring. Using dynamic and slope soaring, it can cover great distances with little exertion. The wandering albatross has a wingspread of almost twelve feet, making it the largest of all flying birds in terms of wingspread. They breed primarily in the Hawaiian Islands, Bonin Islands, and Torishima Islands.

In the late 1800s, millions of short-tailed albatrosses lived or visited one of the Bonins, the "Seven Islands of Izeu." The short-tailed albatross weighs about fifteen pounds and has a wingspan of about seven feet. The Japanese found so many there, they created an industry based on these large birds. They slaughtered the birds for their feathers, oil, and fertilizer.

The islanders built a railway to the top of the island and ran a cableway to the bay. Every man on the island killed between one hundred and two hundred each day, harvesting them for their feather trade. The businessmen of the island killed more than five million albatrosses over a period of less than twenty years. They stuffed their feathers into schooners, cooked their carcasses to obtain the fat, and left their bones to wither in the sun.

Albatrosses were seabirds. They did not understand the need to flee for their lives, and neither did they understand the danger from land predators. As men, intent on their slaughter, approached the unsuspecting fowls, the albatrosses sat patiently on their nests, allowing their massacre with little resistance. For the sake of feather beds, feather pillows, and low-grade fatty fuels, the short-tailed albatross population diminished to only a few dozen immature birds.

Nature eventually had its revenge. The *Audubon Nature Encyclopedia* reported that in 1903 about three hundred humans inhabited the island. Only a few albatrosses remained. While the remaining birds were at sea, the main volcano on Bonin Island erupted, killing all three hundred humans.

Torishima Island was another island where the inhabitants massacred short-tailed albatrosses for years. In 1902 Torishima Island's volcano erupted killing the 125 people working in the feather-harvesting business who were living on the island.

Greed, an intense, selfish desire for wealth or possessions, almost destroyed one entire species of wildlife, the short-tailed albatross. It also ended the life of many workers so caught up in their own self-interest that they failed to notice the impending dangers of island volcanoes.

Newspaper accounts tell of greed among businesses and individuals all too often. The desire to gain wealth and power at the expense of another is rampant. Fortunes are lost due to the unethical practices of those who willingly cheat others out of something of value, but this doesn't have to continue. Conservationists are once again restoring the existence of the short-tailed albatross in the islands of the Pacific Ocean. Good men and women can also restore unselfishness within their own communities.

The antidote for greed is charity. It is benevolence. It is goodwill. As we focus our efforts toward helping others, we create a spontaneous reaction for good. Others see the value of good works and replicate the process. A long tradition of goodwill is established, and we find ourselves living in a community of harmony among all people.

                      Love,

                      Ritchey Marbury

"When prosperity comes, do not use all of it."

—CONFUCIUS

Ask

Dear Missionaries,

I love my children. I want what is best for them. Whatever they ask of me, if it is within my power to give them, I usually will, but only if I feel it will improve their lives. Often I know what they need and get it for them. Other times I wait for them to ask.

Jesus taught that if we know how to give good gifts to our children, how much more shall our Father, who is in Heaven, give good things to them who ask (Matthew 7:11)? James taught the same thing when he wrote, "If any of you lack wisdom, let him ask of God, that giveth to all men liberally, and upbraideth not; and it shall be given him" (James 1:5). He then added, "But let him ask in faith, nothing wavering" (James 1:6).

Joseph Smith received revelations that blessed the world because he asked which church he should join. A leper fell down before Jesus, asked to be made clean, and his wish was granted (Matthew 8:2–3).

Some years ago a tornado swept across Vienna, Georgia. It uprooted trees. It destroyed houses. It created turmoil everywhere. A small child clutched her grandmother's hand and led her into the kitchen. The child said a prayer, then turned to her grandmother and said, "Don't worry. I prayed and asked God to protect us. Everything will be OK."

It was. Fierce winds blew the roof off the house. Neighbors told the mother that the tornado destroyed all the houses in the neighborhood. Frantically the mother rushed home to find her shattered home. It had no roof, but the kitchen was intact. The child and grandmother were safe. A small child asked Heavenly Father for protection, and He answered her prayer.

I spoke with that mother and child years later. The child is grown now, but still remembers how she asked for protection, and how Heavenly Father protected her.

Barney Williams related in a ward council meeting in Albany, Georgia how Heavenly Father answered his prayer. He told how ocean currents swept him and his son several hundred yards from shore while they were swimming at the beach. They treaded water while the current continued pushing them farther and farther from shore. Barney said he thought they both would die. He prayed mightily to Heavenly Father for help.

Help came in an unexpected way. A huge wave seem to lift both of them in the air. It moved steadily toward shore, carrying both of them with it. Before they realized what happened, they stood in only about six inches of water. Grateful for their answer, they walked safely to shore.

Sometimes answers to prayers come in dramatic ways, as in these examples. Sometimes they come in feelings of peace or comfort. Sometimes they come only as feelings. Sometimes the answer is yes, sometimes no, and sometimes wait. The important thing is to ask, and ask in faith. The answer will always come, and it will always be in the way that will give the greatest eternal blessings.

Love,

Ritchey Marbury

"If any of you lack wisdom, let him ask of God, that giveth to all men liberally, and upbraideth not; and it shall be given him. But let him ask in faith, nothing wavering."

—James 1:5–6

Assistant's Presentation

Dear Missionaries,

While looking over my past missionary journals, I found the outline of a presentation by Elders McWhorter and Eve. It teaches worthwhile lessons. Much of the outline seems to come from advice given by Dale Carnegie with additional thoughts and ideas by Elders McWhorter and Eve. Here is part of that outline.

I. Don't criticize, condemn, or complain.
   a. Keys to developing a Zion companionship, Moses 7:18
   b. Baptisms start with love for companion.
   c. "The more perfect one becomes, the less he (or she) is inclined to speak of the imperfections of others."—L. Ray Christenson
   d. "You never would complain of the sharpness of the word of God if you were not under transgression."—Heber C. Kimball

II. Give honest, sincere appreciation.
   a. People can feel when we are honest and sincere.
   b. Give role play showing the importance of honesty.

III. Arouse in the other person an eager want.
   a. It is often said "that if you want to get somewhere, help someone get there first."

  b. "There is a destiny which makes us brothers. None lives for self alone. All that we send into the lives of others comes back into our own."
  c. Baptism is the gateway to Heaven and the Celestial Kingdom.
    i. All will get the opportunity to be baptized in this life or the next.
    ii. Inspired Questions:
      1. One Heavenly Father, one Jesus Christ, so how many churches should there be on the earth?
      2. Jesus Christ is the Savior of the entire world, not just Jerusalem.
      3. How important are the commandments?
      4. Holy Ghost like unto a flashlight.
      5. Importance of Continuous Revelation.
      6. Veil of Forgetfulness.
      7. If Jesus Christ were standing here, what would He ask you to do? (3 Nephi 11:32–34, 37, 38).
      8. If Peter were standing here, what would he ask you to do? (Acts 2:37–38).
IV. Become genuinely interested in other people.
  a. Talk about a common base.
  b. "People don't care how much you know until they know how much you care."
  c. Teach to the people. Don't go over their head or under it.
V. Smile.
  a. "You can recognize the Spirit of Christ within you when you speak to one another or speak of another person with a warm smile instead of with a cold frown."—Theodore M. Burton
  b. Whatever you do, do it with a smile. "Put a smile on your kisser and you will get a kiss on your smiler."
VI. Remember that a person's name is to that person the sweetest and most important sound in any language.
  a. Call on someone to stand up.
  b. Then have everyone repeat his or her name.

VII. Be a good listener. Encourage others to talk about themselves.
   a. What makes a good counselor? When they talk about you and not about I.
   b. Probe to show that you are genuinely interested.
   c. In a discussion, when an investigator is sharing an accomplishment, don't change the focus by talking about yourself.
VIII. Talk in terms of the other person's interests.
   a. Use examples that investigators will understand.
   b. Liken discussions to investigators, as Christ likened principles to the people he was teaching.
IX. Make the other person feel important—and do it sincerely.
   a. Help them answer their own questions. Help them realize the testimony that they have already gained. (Acts 26:27)
   b. Use the example of learning in a classroom.
   c. Use example of "Who is the Father of our Spirits?"

The assistants gave this presentation while training full-time missionaries on how to be more successful on their full-time missions. Not only do these ideas work in the mission field, however; they work in life. They work in church callings, in business, and in your homes. Study and use them. The advice is inspired.

Love,

Ritchey Marbury

"The more perfect one becomes, the less he (or she) is inclined to speak of the imperfections of others."

—L. Ray Christenson

Be One

Dear Missionaries,

"I say unto you, be one; and if ye are not one ye are not mine" (Doctrine and Covenants 38:27. We all belong to each other. We love each other. We pray for each other, and we work together for the perfection of each other. We are all children of our Heavenly Father, and as such, we are all part of one heavenly family.

As each member of our body is part of the whole, each individual is part of the whole family of Christ. Sometimes we mistakenly think that if another is hurt, that doesn't affect us. That is like saying that if our finger is hurt, that doesn't affect how our whole body feels. We are all part of Christ's team and our goal is eternal life for ourselves, our family, and our neighbors. We are one in purpose, and that purpose is to invite all to come unto Christ and be perfected in Him.

It may be easy to say, "Be one," but the doing takes effort. Here are three suggestions:

Begin with forgiving. Be slow to condemn and quick to forgive. We all make mistakes, and we all sometimes hurt others—when we have no idea we have done so. Some people may intentionally do things to hurt, but most times, hurt by others is unintentional and accidental. A cross word here, an unkind word there, and a lifetime of friendship may be destroyed. It doesn't have to be so.

Avoid grudges like you would an infectious disease. Forgiveness heals. Grudges destroy.

Pay attention to how you act in the hard moments. Most of us are kind, loving, and cheerful when we get our way—when the sun is shining. Share your umbrella during rainstorms. You may hit your thumb occasionally as you work with a hammer. When you do, can you say, "Gee, I'm sorry I hit my thumb; I must be more careful next time," or at least keep quiet—or do you scream the first negative thoughts that come into your head? We show who we are by our actions and our words.

Choose the Lord's way with every decision. When we all choose the Lord's way, we act as one. We don't have to learn a multitude of rules. All we have to remember is to love God and love our neighbors. Hartman Rector, many years ago, put that into just two words: "Be nice."

In His great Intercessory Prayer, Jesus prayed, "And now I am no more in the world, but these are in the world, and I come to thee. Holy Father, keep through thine own name those whom thou hast given me, that they may be one, as we are" (John 17:11). Let us all be one in learning and doing those things that will bring eternal life to ourselves and those with whom we have influence.

Love,

Ritchey Marbury

"I say unto you, be one."

—Doctrine and Covenants 38:27

Chimney Rock

BE WISE

Dear Missionaries,

Jacob, the brother of Nephi, gave this council to his brethren, and to all who read his words: "O be wise, what can I say more?" (Jacob 6:12).

Wisdom has various definitions. Some say it is the ability to remember facts. Others say it is the ability to understand complicated mathematical formulas and equations. Many say it is the ability to arrive at common-sense solutions—although common sense seems to be less common every day. Regardless of the definition, wisdom is a desirable attribute.

Since wisdom is so important, why not do what is required to obtain it? Proverbs 9:10 tells us, "The fear of the Lord is the beginning of wisdom." Of all things we learn, knowing and keeping Heavenly Father's commandments brings the greatest benefits. That is because His commandments are designed to make us happy. In fact commandments from our Heavenly Father are really "guidelines for happiness."

We know the Ten Commandments. Are we not happier when we love God, refrain from bowing down to graven images, avoid profanity, rest and keep the Sabbath day holy, respect our parents, avoid murder, avoid adultery, avoid stealing, avoid bearing false witness, and avoid coveting those things that are not ours?

The Lord gave us the Word of Wisdom. It teaches us to avoid tobacco, alcohol, and harmful substances. It teaches us ways to be healthier, and we are happier when we are healthier.

The greatest commandments teach us to love God and our neighbor. Christ teaches us to forgive and to avoid judging others. Think of what a happy world this would be if we all just loved God and our neighbors.

We gain knowledge through studying math, physics, chemistry, philosophy, and other scholarly subjects. We gain wisdom through studying and following Heavenly Father's "guidelines for happiness."

As Jacob said, "O be wise, what can I say more?"

Love,

Ritchey Marbury

"Heavenly Father's commandments are not rules that limit, but guidelines for happiness."

—R<small>ITCHEY</small> M<small>ARBURY</small>

Ben Franklin's New Year Advice

Dear Missionaries,

"Be at war with your vices, at peace with your neighbors, and let every New Year find you a better man." So wrote Benjamin Franklin. Good advice.

Proverbs 6:16 lists seven vices the Lord hates:

(1) a proud look,
(2) a lying tongue,
(3) hands that shed innocent blood,
(4) an heart that deviseth wicked imaginations,
(5) feet that be swift in running to mischief,
(6) a false witness that speaketh lies, and
(7) he that soweth discord among brethren.

To be at war with your vices means to work actively to eliminate them. Alexander Pope wrote these words describing vice:

> Vice is a monster of so frightful mien
> As to be hated needs but to be seen;
> Yet seen too oft, familiar with her face,
> We first endure, then pity, then embrace.

To be at peace with your neighbors, replace vices with virtues. Consider these seven virtues:

(1) humility, being more teachable and recognizing your dependence on a power greater than your own,
(2) honesty, speaking truth at all times,
(3) charity, willingness to give your life, if necessary, to save others
(4) compassion, a kind heart,
(5) service, feet that are swift to do good,
(6) truth seeker, a witness for the truth,
(7) peacemaker, one who seeks to avoid discord.

Work on these virtues. If you perfect only one of them, the New Year will find you a better person.

Love,

Ritchey Marbury

"Conviction is worthless unless it is converted into conduct."

—THOMAS CARLYLE

Captain's Daughter

Dear Missionaries,

The other day I ran across a poem by James T. Fields that reminded me how our Heavenly Father is always near, loving us and protecting us. The poem is called "The Captain's Daughter."

The Captain's Daughter

We were crowded in the cabin,
Not a soul would dare to sleep,—
It was midnight on the waters,
And a storm was on the deep.

'Tis a fearful thing in winter
To be shattered by the blast,
And to hear the rattling trumpet
Thunder, "Cut away the mast!"

So we shuddered there in silence,—
For the stoutest held his breath,
While the hungry sea was roaring
And the breakers talked with Death.

As thus we sat in darkness,
Each one busy with his prayers,
"We are lost!" the captain shouted
As he staggered down the stairs.

But his little daughter whispered,
As she took his icy hand,
"Isn't God upon the ocean,
Just the same as on the land?"

Then we kissed the little maiden
And we spoke in better cheer,
And we anchored safe in harbor
When the morn was shining clear.

Love,

Ritchey Marbury

---

*"Isn't God upon the ocean,
Just the same as on the land?"*

—JAMES T. FIELDS

Character Lessons

Dear Missionaries,

We love Jesus Christ because He loves us. When on this earth, He treated all with love and kindness. As members or full-time missionaries, we influence others by acting nice. I read quotes from Abigail Van Buren, St. Francis de Sales, and Lady Bird Johnson the other day. I include them in this letter as thoughts to consider.

Abigail Van Buren said, "The best index to a person's character is (a) how he treats people who can't do him any good, and (b) how he treats people who can't fight back."

St. Francis de Sales said, "Some men become proud and insolent because they ride a fine horse, wear a feather in their hat or are dressed in a fine suit of clothes. Who does not see the folly of this? If there be any glory in such things, the glory belongs to the horse, the bird, and the tailor."

Lady Bird Johnson said, "Americans have always attached particular value to the word, 'neighbor.' While the spirit of neighborliness was important on the frontier because neighbors were so few, it is even more important now because our neighbors are so many."

Our mission is to invite all to come unto Christ and be perfected in Him. We do that by showing Christlike character, avoiding pride, and being good neighbors.

Love,

Ritchey Marbury

"Goodness is richer than greatness. It consists not in the outward things we do, but in the inward thing we are."

—EDWIN HUBBEL CHAPIN

College For Dessert

Dear Missionaries,

Sherri Daley of Fairfield, Connecticut, wrote in the June 2015 issue of the *AARP Bulletin* about her experience at a dinner just after her son graduated from high school. People at the dinner asked where her son intended to go to college. Sherri was a single mother. She had no idea how she would get tuition money for her son's college. She answered by saying how proud she was of her son but avoided any direct response.

Halfway through dessert a man tapped her on the shoulder. She hardly knew the man and had met him maybe twice.

"You don't have the money to send your son anywhere, do you?"

Sherri did not know how to respond.

The man continued, "My wife and I talked about it. We'll give you the money for college."

Sherri left for the ladies' room. She returned thinking the man was only kidding. He was not. He paid for her son's entire four-year college education. Her son graduated with honors and at age thirty-four is working in real estate investment banking. She later discovered that the man and his wife, every few years, pay for a deserving student to attend college.

We may not all have the finances to pay for another's college tuition, but we can all perform spontaneous acts of kindness.

A smile, a kind word, opening the door for a stranger, writing a letter of encouragement—all these things cost little or nothing but can brighten another's day.

We do not have to use words to be missionaries. Actions say more than words. We teach more effectively by deeds than orations. Often the good we would do, we don't, because we forget to look for good things to do. Why not make it a habit to look for ways to enrich the lives of others? We will enrich our lives, also, in doing so.

Love,

Ritchey Marbury

"Inasmuch as you have done it unto one of the least of these my brethren, ye have done it unto me."

—MATTHEW 25:40

Confession

Dear Missionaries,

Children teach us so much. They are so innocent that they blurt out their feelings with no thought of political correctness or other's reactions to their comments. Their words all too often remind us of how we ought to be and how we really are.

This short poem by Andrew Gillies teaches such a lesson. He titled it "Confession."

> Last night my little boy confessed to me:
> Some childish wrong;
> And kneeling at my knee
> He prayed with tears—
> "Dear God, make me a man
> Like Daddy—wise and strong;
> I know you can."
> Then while he slept
> I knelt beside his bed,
> Confessed my sins,
> And prayed with low-bowed head.

> "Oh God, make me a child
> Like my child here—
> Pure, guileless,
> Trusting Thee with faith sincere."

Love,

Ritchey Marbury

"Whosoever therefore shall humble himself as this little child, the same is greatest in the kingdom of heaven."

—Matthew 18:4

Criticism Or Example

Dear Missionaries,

I sat in a church meeting the other day where one of the participants raved on about how badly the ward operated. He spent twenty minutes of valuable time explaining defect after defect. He went on to complain that everyone seemed to ignore his instruction.

He was right in everything he said, but it made no difference. Others kept doing the same things and making the same mistakes because what he said made them angry. He had antagonized them, and they felt no desire to listen.

Criticism seldom helps. Sometimes the one criticizing hides behind phrases such as "constructive criticism," but all too often the real intent is to belittle the hard work of others because they made a mistake. Often the critic just wants to make himself or herself look good or someone else look bad. Sometimes the critic is just frustrated with the way things are going and legitimately wants to see change for the better, but the tone of the voice or the smirk on the face creates tension and uneasiness.

I know of no monuments built to critics and no great structures built by wrecking companies. Inspectors do find deficiencies that need correcting, but if everyone spent his or her time inspecting and criticizing, no one would do the building. There is a better way.

Jesus Christ said, "Follow me." That seems to be the best way to get things done. Set the example. Look for things done right and praise the effort. Praise progress. Redirect mistakes. Fix the breakdown rather than the blame. Inspire enthusiasm rather than fear. "Show how" works better than "know how."

Love,

Ritchey Marbury

"My life is my message."

—Mahatma Gandhi

David Tarried Still At Jerusalem

Dear Missionaries,

"And it came to pass, after the year was expired, at the time when kings go forth to battle, that David sent Joab, and his servants with him, and all Israel, and they destroyed the children of Ammon, and besieged Rabbah. But David tarried still at Jerusalem" (II Samuel 11:1).

Instead of being on the battlefield, David took a walk upon the roof of his house. He observed a beautiful woman washing herself. He enquired after the woman. Her name was Bathsheba, the wife of Uriah the Hittite.

David sent messengers and took her. She came unto him. He committed adultery with her, and she conceived. Bathsheba sent and told David she was with child, and David tried to cover his sin.

In his effort to cover his sin, David sent for Uriah. Uriah was on the battlefield where David should have been. When Uriah arrived, David told him to go to his house. Uriah, however, slept at the door of the king's house and did not go to his own house. When David enquired why, Uriah answered, "The servants of my lord, are encamped in the open fields; shall I then go into mine house, to eat and to drink?...as thou livest and as thy soul livest, I will not do this thing."

David tried again to cover his sin by telling Uriah to stay a day longer. David invited Uriah to eat and drink with him and made Uriah drunk. Uriah, still, refused to go to his house to be with his wife.

David then wrote a letter to his servant Joab. He told Joab to send Uriah to the forefront of the hottest battle and retire from him, that he may be smitten and die. Joab did, Uriah died, and now David was guilty not only of adultery but also murder.

David's tragedy shows the danger of not being where you should be when you should be. It was the time when kings should go forth to battle. David was king. He should have gone forth to battle, but he tarried in Jerusalem. The results were traumatic.

The spirit of the Lord is always where it should be. The Holy Ghost is our protector when we go where the Lord directs. When we tarry, we forfeit that protection.

It was time for kings to go to battle, but David tarried still at Jerusalem—and he lost blessings that could and should have been his.

Love,

Ritchey Marbury

"There are no successful sinners. All must one day stand before God and be judged."

—HAROLD B. LEE

Devastation And Recovery

Dear Missionaries,

Natural disasters seem to increase every year. The loss of life, property, and wealth is devastating. Depression comes with the disasters, but comfort comes from the way so many gather together to help. I wrote this sonnet about such efforts.

Devastation And Recovery

So often when we see the devastation
Of hurricanes, tornados, wind, and rain,
Of earthquakes and storm surges and the pain
Of millions homeless all throughout the nation,

We wonder if we ever can recover
From loss of power, property, and life,
From loss of son and daughter, husband, wife,
And other losses we may soon discover.

But then we see the help come rushing in
From north and south and also east and west,
Both men and women work and do their best
To help them all recover and begin

*To know what counts. It's how we'll all endeavor
To share life's tragedies and joys together.*

Love,

Ritchey Marbury

"We all have strength enough to bear the misfortunes of others."

—L<small>A</small> R<small>OCHEFOUCAULD</small>

Church Members Helping Clean Up After Albany

Dick Beason's New Year's Resolutions

Dear Missionaries,

While serving as executive secretary to the Georgia District Presidency, Dick Beason wrote a fun and thought-provoking article for their January 1971 monthly newsletter. Here it is.

MY NEW YEAR'S RESOLUTIONS

As I reflect on the past year's imperfections, I realize that many of my problems were caused by my Number One enemy—me. With resolve, I have decided that there are several things which I shall do this next year, which were not done last year. First, I believe I will try reading the scriptures on a regular basis. All have found it difficult to schedule scripture reading in their days, therefore I propose a plan called "page a day," where by the reader studies and meditates on only one page of scripture per day, minimum. Of course more than one page a day is acceptable, but each should read at least one page. I bet that the scriptures would come "alive" for anyone who pursued this plan.

Next, I plan to slide off the bed each morning in a kneeling position. Right now, pause and feel your knees. Are there praying callouses on your kneecaps? Knee work is essential in spiritual physical fitness. Who wants a flabby spirit shambling around inside of himself?

I have been trying the page a day plan and have uncovered the cause of the fall of the Nephite culture from this daily study. It seems that the whole root of the Nephite problem was that they failed to do their home teaching. If you don't believe me, study the scriptures and see for yourself!

In one chapter, I read where Brother Omni didn't visit his assigned families for a year. As a result, all fell into disbelief and started worshipping Baal. Take for instance Brother Ammon, who, because he was not home taught, decided to contribute to the local chariot maker instead of to the Church. Ammon bought a brand new, 325 BC, wide-tracked, wide oval polyglass tired, four in the floor, three horse power chariot instead of paying his tithing, and was last seen dwindling into unbelief all over the countryside.

This story came right after the one which told of the plight of the saints in the City of Bountiful, who had become prideful and stiff-necked, wearing costly clothing and deeming themselves over their brethren. This all happened because they couldn't find out that this was a "no-no" because their Branch Library Program had faltered and no one could look up the proper references. It seems that Sister Shamalahazbaz had been called by the bishop to be the librarian for the ward, and because of her outside of the home and Church activities had never gotten the program started. The ward was last observed dwindling into darkness, having failed to pay regular installments to the Gospel Light and Power Company.

The ward was having budget problems, too. As I continued reading, I learned that the Lamanites had invaded and captured most all of the farmland around Bountiful City and had laid siege to the town. Again, there were more problems because Brother Mathimimorishezah, President of the Elder's Quorum, didn't know about the family food storage program (because of the library program) and had failed to tell the members of the quorum to store food. At last glance, Brother Ammon, who had purchased the 325 BC chariot instead of paying his tithing, was busily engaged in trying various techniques in cooking his chariot to try to feed his hungry family. Now it's Ammon's waistline that's dwindling, and he can't believe that either.

Meanwhile, Brother Shameel, on active duty on the frontier with the Nephite Army, was having a morale problem. The ward executive secretary was derelict in his duties and had forgotten to send clay tablets regularly to Brother Shemeel, telling him of the news of the ward and encouraging him to lead a cheerfully wholesome life. Worse than this, because of the secretary's dereliction of duty, all of the ward service men had been forgotten during the last sacrifice days and none had received other packages from home or the annual greeting plates of brass. Well, anyway, they were just service men and they weren't around to see; besides, there were more pressing problems around the city. Anyway, hadn't that powerful political leader, Gadianton, promised to bring the troops home, reduce taxes, increase welfare, provide jobs for all, reduce inflation, and establish the eight-hour work week?

So you see, brethren, I have gained a whole lot from my resolutions. I believe that I will continue the page a day plan and hope that I can get everyone to do his duties. Before I do anything, I've got to see the eye doctor to get him to remove this bothersome beam which is in my eye, because it has ruined my vision. I keep seeing motes in other folk's eyes because of it.

What are your New Year's Resolutions?

—Richard W. Beason

Thank you, Dick, for a thought provoking and amusing account of your New Year's Resolutions. I enjoyed it when you wrote it in

January 1971. I hope those of you who read this letter enjoy it now, as much as we did then.

                Love,

                Ritchey Marbury

"Are there praying callouses on your kneecaps?"

—RICHARD W. BEASON

Donuts And Temptation

Dear Missionaries,

The other day an office worker brought a batch of hot, fresh donuts into my office. The smell was tempting, and the fact that they were hot and fresh made my mouth water. Still, I was on a diet and decided not to partake.

The next day another batch of donuts appeared. I looked hard at the donuts but decided that I wanted to be slim more than I wanted a treat.

Two days later, there was another batch. I walked over to the donuts, picked one up, and put it down. I would not give in to temptation.

The following Monday morning, the worker placed a box of donuts right in the middle of my desk. I thought, "Only one won't hurt." I ate one. It was so delicious I ate another. Then I shared the rest of the donuts with the office staff.

Isn't that the way Satan works? First, he temps us, and we resist. He entices us again, and we resist again. Then we allow ourselves to think about how much we would enjoy just a little indulgence. After all, we are strong, and one time won't hurt. After all, we are not really breaking any commandments. Some things are just suggestions.

We are tempted one more time, and after so many temptations, we succumb. Then we do it again. Then we attempt to get others to partake with us.

The Lord warns to flee from temptation. He understands that temptations are hard but teaches that He "will not suffer you to be tempted above that ye are able; but will with the temptation also make a way to escape, that ye may be able to bear it" (1 Corinthians 10:13). He teaches in James 4:7 to "resist the devil, and he will flee from you."

Often you are strong when first tempted. Why not get rid of the temptation when you are strong by staying away from those things that tempt you to do sinful or even unwise things? Your power to resist is stronger at the beginning. As you become more familiar with a temptation, you endure it and then embrace it. Then, if you are not careful, you encourage others to share in your unwise acts.

I am just a little overweight, and I love to eat donuts. Maybe just one won't hurt—or will it?

Love,

Ritchey Marbury

"The only safe ground is so far from danger as it is possible to get."

—Heber J. Grant

Dreams And Prayers

Dear Missionaries,

Once a sister missionary had a serious illness preventing her from continuing to serve. When she left her area, we needed to find a replacement quickly. Since the assistants and I had no idea what to do, we presented our need to the Lord in prayer. The feeling we had was to ask a stake missionary to serve as a temporary companion to the remaining full-time missionary. We had a particular sister in mind.

At that time the Church allowed the stake to call stake missionaries to serve with the full-time missionaries. One sister stake missionary had completed her service a few months before, and we knew she lived on a limited budget. Both the assistants and I felt impressed that she was the one the Lord wanted, but I was reluctant to ask.

The assistants and I prayed again and still felt we should contact her. We knew her stake president would agree for her to serve. However, we did not want to cause an undue financial burden to her or her family. After further prayer, we made the decision. I asked the assistants to drive to her home and discuss the matter with her. It would not be a calling, since that must come from her stake president. This provided a way she could say no without refusing a calling.

The assistants drove to her home and knocked on the door. She answered and invited them in. As soon as they sat down, the sister spoke.

"I know why you are here, and the answer is yes. I had a dream last night and saw you sitting in the chair you are sitting in now. You are here to ask if I would serve again as a stake missionary companion to one of the full-time sister missionaries in the mission. The answer is yes."

The assistants returned and told me what happened. Within days her stake president and bishop approved the request, and the sister began serving She served with distinction. She uplifted her full-time missionary companion and brought the Spirit of the Lord into every home she entered.

Love,

Ritchey Marbury

"Trust in the Lord with all thine heart; and lean not unto thine own understanding. In all thy ways acknowledge Him and He shall direct thy paths."

—Proverbs 3:5–6

Easter Lily

Dear Missionaries,

Five-year-old Amy stared at a white flower on the kitchen table early one Easter morning. The flower had not yet fully opened and assumed a trumpet-shaped appearance.

"I know why the Easter lily is shaped like a trumpet today," said Amy. Her eyes sparkled with faith. "It's showing us that Jesus rose from the grave and Heavenly Father is calling Him home."

"Do you know why the lily is white?" asked her mother.

"Sure I do," replied Amy. "It's because Jesus was pure and without sin. If I follow Jesus, I can be pure and without sin, too."

The Easter lily graces many homes in the spring, especially at Easter. This spring-blooming flower symbolizes life, purity, hope, and the spiritual meaning of Easter. It symbolizes a new birth and a new beginning. Some call it "the white-robed apostle of hope."

There are many legends about the Easter lily. One says these lilies sprang up from Christ's sweat in His final hours of agony in the Garden of Gethsemane. Another says that when Eve left the Garden of Eden, she shed tears of repentance, and lilies grew from those tears—the message being that true repentance is the beginning of beauty.

Some legends say white lilies grew where drops of blood fell from Jesus's body at His crucifixion. Early paintings depict the Angel Gabriel offering a branch of pure white lilies to the

Virgin Mary, announcing she will be the mother of Jesus. Other paintings show saints bringing vases full of white lilies to Mary and the Christ Child.

Jesus taught in Matthew 6:28–29, "And why take ye thought for raiment? Consider the lilies of the field, how they grow; they toil not, neither do they spin: And yet I say unto you, that even Solomon in all his glory was not arrayed like one to these."

A World War I soldier named Louis Houghton brought the Bermuda lily, now known as the Easter lily, to the southern coast of Oregon in 1919. He brought bulbs of these lilies in a suitcase and distributed them to his friends and family. This area along the California-Oregon border produces more than 90 percent of the bulbs grown for the potted Easter lily market.

Greenhouse growers receive the bulbs in the fall, place them in pots, and store them in nonfreezing cool temperatures. They need about a thousand hours of moist cool to bloom. Once they sprout, the growers monitor the temperature to speed up or slow down the growth so that the flowers produce during the Easter season. The plants are sometimes called "wheelbarrow crops," as they are often moved between warm and cold greenhouses to control their availability for Easter. Growers often track growth by recording the rate of leaf unfolding, a technique known as "leaf counting."

Easter is a time of hope, excitement, and joy. It is a time we are grateful for the knowledge that life is everlasting. It is a special time when we remember our love for the Savior, Jesus Christ, and the love and sacrifice He gave that we might not have to suffer as He did. The Easter lily is a symbol to that love. It reminds us that as we believe in Christ and follow His example, we may return to Him and our Heavenly Father and live in joy and happiness with them forever.

Love,

Ritchey Marbury

"Easter says you can put truth in a grave, but it won't stay there."

—Clarence W. Hall

Every Member A Missionary

Dear Missionaries,

Moroni 10:34 teaches us to "come unto Christ and be perfected in Him." This is the mission of the Church, to invite all to come unto Christ and be perfected in Him. It has three dimensions: (1) Proclaim the gospel. (2) Perfect the saints. (3) Redeem the dead. We are missionaries to nonmembers as we proclaim the gospel. We are missionaries to members as we perfect the saints. We are missionaries to the those who passed on before us as we redeem the dead.

David O. McKay taught many times during his presidency, "Every member a missionary." You know that, but you may feel you do not know how. Many of you are full-time missionaries or soon will be. Many of you are return missionaries, and all full-time missionaries will someday be return missionaries. Others of you never served a full-time mission. Still, many ask the question, "As a member, not now serving a full-time mission, what is the best way for me to participate in missionary service?"

Elder Franklin D. Richards answered that question many years ago. He taught three ways.

First, Elder Richards taught to set a righteous example. As explained in Matthew 5:16, "Let your light so shine before men, that they may see your good works, and glorify your Father which is in Heaven." To nonmembers and members alike, this means to set an example of love, service, and kindness. When a lady stooped to wipe the tears from a crying child, the child asked if the lady was God.

"No," the lady replied, "just one of His children."

"I knew you had to be some kin," said the child.

Your righteous example proclaims the gospel to both members and nonmembers. Your example of temple attendance and maintaining a current temple recommend helps in the vital work of redeeming the dead.

Second, Elder Richards taught to ask golden questions. The most common question is, "What do you know about the Mormon Church? Would you like to know more?" Another question taught by Elder Hartman Rector, Jr. is, "Do you like to read? If I gave you a book containing the actual account of the visit of Jesus Christ to America, would you read it?"

When they answer yes, get their name, address, and telephone number, and give it to the full-time missionaries.

You help perfect the saints and do missionary work for the dead by asking members or nonmembers, "What do you know about your ancestors?" You can then tell them about the genealogy program of the Church. You can help them understand how they can have their family with them forever.

Third, Elder Richards taught to ask friends and neighbors to attend church and church activities with you. This includes your less active friends. Sacrament is easy. Every ward and branch holds sacrament meetings. Sometimes friends and neighbors will go. Often they will not.

Sometimes the easiest way to get others to church is through fun activities. Block parties, family home evenings, dinner socials, golf or fishing outings, parties for special events such as Christmas and Halloween, talent shows—all these are fun and nonthreatening events to sometimes shy or hesitant individuals.

Invite members with current temple recommends to attend the temple with you and together perform temple ordinances. One family in Albany, Georgia, purchased a van, which they drive to the temple once a month, taking as many with them as their van has capacity to carry.

The opportunity for missionary service is a blessing for every member.

Love,

Ritchey Marbury

"Every member a missionary."

—David O. McKay

Examine Yourself

Dear Missionaries,

As full-time or member missionaries, we often have the opportunity to teach others what is right and what is wrong. We testify to the truthfulness of the gospel, bear witness to the divinity of Jesus Christ, and encourage others to follow His example. Perhaps a little self-examination will be good for us all.

When choosing someone to trust, could you trust yourself? Do you speak as well of your friends when they are absent as when they are present? Would you like to work for yourself? Would you hire yourself? Is your word as good as your written contract? If you found a lost wallet or purse that contained more than one hundred dollars in cash, would you seek out the owner? Would you pay a person as fair a price for something he or she must sell as you would if he or she had no need to sell?

Would you like to be your own home or visiting teacher? When you teach a class, would you like to be one of the students? If you make a mistake, would you like to be your own judge? Would you help the poor as quickly as you would help the rich? Would you like to live with yourself? If there were no courts, jails, or disgrace, would you ever take what you knew you should not take? If there were no locks, would you go where you knew you had no right to go?

Sometimes it is good to look at ourselves as honestly as if we were someone else. Doing so is good advice and may make us better people.

Love,

Ritchey Marbury

"Advice is seldom welcome. Those who need it most, like it least."

—S<small>AMUEL</small> J<small>OHNSON</small>

Faith Is Like A Muscle

Dear Missionaries,

Faith is like a muscle. It gets stronger when you use it and weaker when you ignore it. Faith precedes blessings. We have faith that planting will produce a harvest. We have faith that studying will produce learning. We have faith that work will produce income.

We demonstrate our faith by our works. James 2:19–20 tells us, "Thou believest that there is one God; thou doest well: the devils also believe and tremble. But wilt thou know, O vain man, that faith without works is dead." Faith and works together bring us to our desired destination.

Work without faith, all too often, also leads to discontent and discouragement. Often failure to finish is due to a lack of faith. Faith and work are like a team of oars. Row with only the right oar, and you move in circles to the right. Row with only the left oar, and you move in circles to the left. Row with both oars, and you move forward. Approach your destination with both faith and works, and you succeed.

Love,

Ritchey Marbury

"I will listen to anyone's convictions, but pray keep your doubts to yourself."

—GOETHE

Faith Works

Dear Missionaries,

Sometimes we do things because we believe that doing them will bring desired results. We aren't sure. We just believe. We have faith, and that is all right. Alma said, "Faith is not to have a perfect knowledge of things; therefore if you have faith ye hope for things which are not seen, which are true" (Alma 32:21). We justify our faith by our works.

James taught us in James 2:20 that "faith without works is dead." I planted a garden last week. I have done this for many years. Some years I have a good harvest. Some years I don't. The results are based on the work I put into the garden, both when I plant, and as I continue to work the garden during the growing season.

I always have faith that the garden will produce a wonderful crop of vegetables, but it sometimes doesn't. When it doesn't, it is usually due to a lack of work on my part.

Some years I don't prepare the soil properly. Some years I don't keep it watered and fertilized. Other years I don't keep it weeded. When I do the work, I receive the harvest. When I don't, the crop fails.

Do we expect knowledge without study, good health without proper diet and exercise, or income without work? As we exercise our faith, it becomes stronger, and our ability to accomplish increases. We develop faith the same way we develop any other skill. We study, practice, and work at it. It is like a muscle; it get stronger the more we use it.

Faith in Jesus Christ comes by scripture study, prayer, and fasting. It comes by living what we profess to believe. It comes by work. As our faith increases, our ability to do good works increases. Isn't that what life is about?

Love,

Ritchey Marbury

"God is the silent partner in all great enterprises."

—ABRAHAM LINCOLN

Faster Than A Speeding Horse

Dear Missionaries,

For nearly six thousand years, the speed of a horse limited the speed of civilization. No matter how many conquests by armies, no matter how many riches or possessions, the speed of civilization could not exceed between 35 and 38 miles per hour—the speed of a horse.

From the fall of Adam and Eve around 4000 BC, to the completion of the Great Pyramid of Giza around 2560 BC, Joseph standing before Pharaoh in Egypt around 1715 BC, and the beginning of the Shang Dynasty in China at 1600 BC, humanity was limited to the speed of a horse—somewhere between 35 and 38 miles per hour.

Solomon reigned as king between 1015 BC until 975 BC. All considered him the wisest king who ever lived, and possibly the richest. He built a magnificent temple, a mansion for his own home, and ornate structures all over his kingdom. He must have ridden on beautiful chariots made from the finest materials. Still, he could move no faster than a horse—between 35 and 38 miles per hour.

In fourteen hundred and ninety two, Columbus sailed the ocean blue. When he arrived on land, he could still travel no more than the speed of a horse. April 18, 1775, the night of the midnight ride of Paul Revere, as Revere raced through every Middlesex village and town, the fastest he could go was the speed of his horse—somewhere between 35 and 38 miles per hour.

After six thousand years of humanity limited to the speed of a horse, something remarkable happened. On April 6, 1830, the Lord established His church, the Church of Jesus Christ of Latter-day Saints. This began the restoration of all things, and the beginning of travel faster than a speeding horse.

May 30, 1830, Peter Cooper designed and tested a new steam engine. Three months later, his steam engine raced a horse. Although the horse won, for a short period the steam engine moved faster than the horse, exceeding 39 miles per hour. By July 31, 1831, the B&O Railroad replaced all horses with steam locomotives.

By April of 1865, at the end of the Civil War in the United States, the North had trains running up to 60 miles per hour. By 1905 some trains could run up to 127 miles per hour.

December 17, 1903, Orville and Wilbur Wright, near Kitty Hawk, North Carolina, made the first successful flight of a heavier-than-air, self-propelled aircraft. The propeller-driven airplane stayed aloft for twelve seconds. It covered 120 feet. Humans were no longer limited to travel over land or sea. Like birds, humans could now travel in the air.

On October 14, 1947, Chuck Yeager, flying the experimental Bell X-1 at an altitude of forty-five thousand feet became the first human to break the sound barrier, traveling more than 768 miles per hour.

As a boy, I thrilled to stories of Superman flying "faster than a speeding bullet." Humans broke the Superman barrier on Friday, September 21, 1956. Thomas W. Attridge Jr. flew an F11F Tiger on a test flight over the Atlantic Ocean. He entered a shallow dive and fired a four-second burst of gunfire from an altitude of thirteen thousand feet. He entered a steeper dive and fired his cannons again at seven thousand feet. The plane rattled as bullets ripped through part of his airplane. Traveling at about 880 miles per hour, the Tiger flew into its own bullets. Like Superman, my childhood comic book hero, he was literally traveling "faster than a speeding bullet."

"That's one small step for (a) man, one giant leap for mankind." Neil Armstrong broadcasted these words Monday, July 21, 1969. That day he became the first human to step onto the moon, followed by Astronaut Buzz Aldrin. In order to escape earth's gravity, a speed exceeding the escape velocity of earth was required—a speed greater than twenty-five thousand miles per hour.

When the Lord restored His church, He also opened the windows of knowledge and opportunity. He improved not only our ability to travel at high speeds, but also our ability to communicate with anyone anywhere. We have the opportunity to use this knowledge for good, but opportunity is only valid when we use it. Because of the restoration of speed and knowledge, we have the ability to teach all nations, kindred, tongues, and people. We have the opportunity to teach the blessings available to all because of the restoration of Christ's church and His many sacrifices for us. We can do so by our words, our deeds, and our prayers.

Love,

Ritchey Marbury

"Opportunity is only valid when we use it."

—Ritchey Marbury

Folded Napkin

Dear Missionaries,

An old Hebrew tradition tells the significance of a folded napkin left on the table. While the master dined, Jewish boys, in the time of Christ, watched as the master finished eating. The master rose from the table, cleaned his fingers and mouth, and left—but not before signaling with the napkin. If the master wadded the napkin and tossed it on the table, the servant knew the master had finished the meal. The servant could then clean.

Sometimes, however, the master left the table before completing the meal. The servant needed to know if the master was finished in order to know whether to clean. There was a sign. If the master planned to come back, he would carefully fold the napkin and place it neatly beside the plate. This said, "I am coming back."

After Christ's crucifixion, on the first day of the week, Mary Magdalene went to Jesus's sepulcher. He was gone. Someone had rolled away the stone blocking the entrance. Mary ran to tell some of the disciples. Together they returned to the sepulcher. Simon Peter went inside. He saw the linen clothes, but the napkin that had wrapped the head of Jesus did not lie with them. It was wrapped together in a place by itself.

Only a few days earlier, Jesus comforted His disciples with these words, "Let not your heart be troubled: ye believe in God, believe also in me. In my Father's house are many mansions: if it were not so, I would have told you. I go to prepare a place for you. And if I go and prepare a place for you, I will come again, and receive you unto myself; that where I am, there ye may be also" (John 14:1–3).

The folded napkin said in an unmistakable way, "I will come again."

Love,

Ritchey Marbury

"And if I go and prepare a place for you, I will come again, and receive you unto myself; that where I am, there ye may be also"

—JOHN 14:3

Forever Family

Dear Missionaries,

While serving as stake president of the Columbus, Georgia, stake, a family asked for an interview. This wonderful family loved each other and wished to be together forever. The father, however, had left. He had been unrighteous, and did not seem to be the kind of father or husband worthy of such a great family. I will not mention any names here, because of the nature of this interview and the subsequent events.

During the interview, I asked the family what they wanted most. The child replied, "We want to be a forever family."

I told the family to keep praying and Heavenly Father would answer their prayers. I did not promise the family would get back together, but I did promise an answer to their prayers.

Meanwhile, unknown to me or the family, the father had moved to Florida. He related his story to me in a later interview.

The father wandered one day into the Church parking lot. He approached a man working with flowers at the front of the Church. The father believed the man to be the gardener. For reasons the father knew not, he discussed his family situation with the gardener. The gardener suggested he go inside and talk with the bishop. He did.

The bishop told him to return to his family and he would see good things happen. Then the bishop asked what made this father decide to speak with him. When the father said the gardener suggested it, the bishop replied, "What gardener? We have no gardener working here."

They both looked outside and found no one. I wish I could remember more details, but I felt the events were too sacred to record, and I do not remember any more details.

I do remember the most important fact, however. I later had an interview with the family. The entire family, including the repentant father, were found worthy to enter the temple and be sealed as a forever family. They did so.

The child said to me later, "I prayed that our family would be together forever, and now we will be. We are a forever family."

Love,

Ritchey Marbury

"God has given us no greater blessing than that of belonging to a loving and loyal family—and it will be so, always and forever."

—Richard L. Evans

Forgotten

Dear Missionaries,

A fellow worker died yesterday. It was early Tuesday morning, July 28, 2015. His name was Lance Calloway, and he was my friend. He had no known living family. He was an only child. He never married, so he had no children. His parents died many years ago. He walked to work every day since he had no car. He had practically no assets, so the funeral home is holding his body until someone agrees to pay his funeral expenses. He worked in the water department for the City of Cordele, Georgia, and was little known anywhere else. It seems as if he is already forgotten.

Lance once told me about his neighbor who needed food and clothing. He said he gave him what little food and extra clothing he had and wished he could have given more. Still, Lance gave what he had. He worked hard, was always dependable, and made it a point to arrive early to work and stay until he finished his job.

In the years to come, Lance may or may not be remembered on this earth, but Heavenly Father knows him and will remember him forever. In fact He will remember all of us forever. Jesus taught, "Are not five sparrows sold for two farthings, and not one of them is forgotten before God? But even the very hairs of your head are all numbered. Fear not therefore: ye are of more value than many sparrows" (Luke 12:6–7). Isaiah taught how God reminds us that "thou shalt not be forgotten of me" (Isaiah 44:21).

Heavenly Father knows all of us, and none are forgotten. As missionaries we all have the opportunity to help others remember Heavenly Father—and every member is a missionary.

You help others remember Heavenly Father as you teach how to love one another. You help as you teach the importance of daily prayer and scripture study. You help as you teach about family history and temple service. Heavenly Father always remembers us, so may we always remember Him.

Love,

Ritchey Marbury

"And now, O man, remember, and perish not."

—MOSIAH 4:30

PS

Lance's fellow workers did remember him and held a memorial service for him on August 17, 2015. They found a cousin who knew of Lance's history. Lance was the son of Davis Calvin Calloway and Sarah Bertha Walden Calloway. He worked for the City of Cordele, Georgia, for forty-five years. Lance was buried next to his parents.

Glen L. Rudd Teaches

Dear Missionaries,

Glen L. Rudd was mission president of the Florida Mission during the three years just prior to the day Fonda and I were baptized, September 4, 1969. He never gave up on us before and after our baptism. He encouraged us to remain faithful to the gospel and was one of our witnesses when we were later sealed together in the Salt Lake Temple for time and all eternity on June 16, 1971. Elder Harold B. Lee performed the ceremony.

President Rudd and I have the same birthday. His birthday is May 18, 1918. My birthday is May 18, 1938. He just came to this earth twenty years before me—probably so he could help me learn more about the true gospel of Jesus Christ. Today, some forty-seven years after our baptism, he still sometimes contacts me to encourage and uplift. I am grateful to such a wonderful man ninety-eight years young.

President Rudd keeps meticulous records and writes many stories. He publishes his own scrap & and notebooks containing stories and words of wisdom, none of which are copyrighted. Here is one of them.

ABOU BEN THE SECOND

It was a town meeting where everybody knew everybody else. There had been a meeting of the boys of junior high age, some 65 in number. The man in charge had asked them to write down the name of the man in their town they most admired, the man they would most want to be like when they grew up.

Individual fathers, of course, were the most often named, but the man who got the most votes was a hardware dealer we shall call Jim Bentley. He got 13 votes.

The next morning the man who had asked the question called on the hardware merchant. He spread 13 pieces of paper on the counter. All had Bentley's name on them, though it was often misspelled. "What do you see here, Jim?" he asked.

"Some kinda grubby pieces of paper with my name on 'em," the merchant said, "Where'd you get 'em? What they for?"

"Ever hear of Abou Ben Adhem, Jim, the gent whose name led all the rest?"

"Yep. Can recite it, too, that poem about him. Learned it in sixth grade."

"Well, Jim, you're sort of Abou Ben the Second. I asked my 65 boys last night who in this town they would most like to be when they grow up, and a fellow named Jim Bentley led all the rest. What do you think of that?"

The man in front of him turned white and clutched the counter for support.

"What do I think of it?" he said at last. "I think it is too great a responsibility for any man to live up to, but it is the highest honor that has ever come to me. I am not worthy of it."

The man who told the story said, "I knew that man. Many times he told me how that little incident had affected his life. He said that never thereafter could he do a single thing without seeing 13 pairs of eyes looking at him from every corner and fence row as if for guidance. Would they be better or worse men if they imitated him? It was too great a responsibility, but he was going to measure up to it if he possibly could.

Come to think of it, it's quite a responsibility if only one boy picks you as the man he would want to be like when he grows up.

For me Glen L. Rudd is one of those men, along with other great men like my father, Bob Oates, and Clifford Clive. Thanks, President Rudd, for being my friend for so many years. May all who read this have friends like you, a young man of ninety-eight years.

Love,

Ritchey Marbury

"In every happening there is a story: Find it! Write it down! Use it"

—Glen L. Rudd

PS

Some of you may have never heard the poem, "Abou Ben Adhem." For that reason it is added below:

Abou Ben Adhem
By James Henry Leigh Hunt

Abou Ben Adhem (may his tribe increase!)
Awoke one night from a deep dream of peace,
And saw, within the moonlight in his room,
Making it rich, and like a lily in bloom,

An angel writing in a book of gold:—
Exceeding peace had made Ben Adhem bold,
And to the Presence in the room he said
"What writest thou?"—The vision raised its head,
And with a look made of all sweet accord,
Answered "The names of those who love the Lord."
"And is mine one?" said Abou. "Nay, not so,"
Replied the angel. Abou spoke more low,
But cheerly still, and said "I pray thee, then,
Write me as one that loves his fellow men."

The angel wrote, and vanished. The next night
It came again with a great wakening light,
And showed the names whom love of God had blessed,
And lo! Ben Adhem's name led all the rest.

God Is Not Mocked

Dear Missionaries,

A young man stood defiantly before the judge. Police had arrested him for bribery; he stood trial and awaited sentencing. He brought a character witness to his trial hoping to obtain a reduced sentence. The character witness testified the man tithed 10 percent of his ill-gotten gain.

"What?" asked the judge. "You tried to bribe God, too?"

According to reports, one evening President Woodrow Wilson received a call from an acquaintance in the middle of the night. He told President Wilson that one of the president's appointees had suddenly died. The acquaintance expressed sadness for the death, and then proceeded with the real purpose of his call.

"Do you think I might take his place?"

President Wilson paused and then replied, "It's all right with me, if it's all right with the undertaker."

Heavenly Father knows our hearts. We reap what we sow, regardless of our excuses. Better to do right the first time, but if not, repent quickly, pay the price, and proceed to do right from that time forward. Heavenly Father loves us all. He knows we are not perfect and is quick to forgive. However, repentance must be real. He knows our heart and mind. He gives us the strength to do right if we just ask with real intent.

Love,

Ritchey Marbury

"Be not deceived; God is not mocked: for whatsoever a man soweth, that shall he also reap."

—GALATIANS 6:7

Happiness Is Like Pages In Your Journal

Dear Missionaries,

"Men are, that they might have joy" (2 Nephi 2:25). "And the angel said unto them, Fear not: for, behold, I bring you good tidings of great joy, which shall be to all people" (Luke 2: 10). "If ye know these things, happy are ye if ye do them" (John 13:17).

Happiness is a blessing from God. He delights when we are happy. In fact, He gave us commandments that teach us happiness. Commandments from God in reality are simply "guidelines for happiness." Happiness is also a habit. Someone said that we are about as happy as we make up our minds to be.

Happiness is good for you. Your brain at positive performs significantly better than your brain at negative, neutral, or stressed. When you are happy, your intelligence rises, your creativity rises, your energy level rises, and business outcomes improve.

This letter is about how to develop happiness habits. When you are happy, you do better at work, you make better grades at school, and you have a more peaceful home life.

You develop habits by repeating behaviors for a consecutive period—many say twenty-one days. Here are six behaviors that, when converted into habits, will help you stay a happy person. You can remember them by remembering that happiness is like PAGES in your Journal.

"P" is for Prayer. It really works. Some call it meditation, but it is more than that; it is conversing with your Heavenly Father. Develop the habit of morning and evening family prayers and random regular personal prayers.

When my son was a small boy, he got lost one afternoon. After only a few minutes, Fonda and I found him beside an alley only a couple of blocks from our home. As soon as he saw us, he remarked, "What took you so long? I got lost, so I prayed that Heavenly Father would help you find me, and He did."

"A" is for Acts of Kindness. Acts of kindness bless both the giver and the receiver, and the giver is often the most blessed.

Our family always enjoyed playing Home Evening Phantom. Often we would prepare small gifts of cookies for a family we knew. We would wrap the gifts and include a card saying, "From the Home Evening Phantom."

Just as it got dark, our children would place the gift on their doorstep, ring the bell, and hide. Often we laughed to ourselves when, at church the next Sunday, the family told others about their surprise gifts.

"G" is for Gratitude. Gratitude expressed three or more times every day, helps you become more appreciative of your blessings and less concerned about your misfortunes.

My friend, Jeff Morrow, was a great example. He developed a disease called myasthenia gravis, a rare disease of the nervous system that hinders a person's mobility. He spent many nights in the hospital receiving blood transfusions and other uncomfortable and sometimes painful treatments. With all his pain and discomfort, he continually thanked his wife, his children, and his nurses for the care and treatment they give him. I never heard Jeff complain about his condition, but I often heard him say how happy he was that he had so many friends and such a good family.

"E" is for Exercise. Practically every health publication tells the benefits of exercise. Exercise improves blood circulation. It tones muscles and boosts energy. Exercise improves health, and healthier people are happier.

"S" is for Scripture Study. "Feast upon the words Christ," said Nephi (2 Nephi 2:3). Since he did not say, "nibble," I suppose he meant to study and ponder Christ's words. Since Heavenly Father sent Christ into the world to bless all who heed His teachings, daily study of His teachings is the way to happiness. His teachings are in the scriptures.

"J" is for Journal. Reading positive and uplifting experiences helps you to relive them; therefore, keep a journal of your positive, spiritual, and uplifting experiences, so you can relive and remember them. True, journals may include the sad experiences of life, but when the focus of your journal is on the positive, you will have a more positive life.

Although life is everlasting, our life on this earth is finite. Why not make it a happy one?

      Love,

      Ritchey Marbury

"True happiness comes only from making others happy."

      —DAVID O. MCKAY

Harold B. Lee's Example

Dear Missionaries,

Harold B. Lee served as president of the Church of Jesus Christ of Latter-day Saints for seventeen months. Before that, he served as a member of the Quorum of the Twelve Apostles for thirty-one years. He served as one of the Salt Lake County commissioners. He served as president of the Pioneer Stake in Salt Lake City, Utah. Due to the welfare program that he established while stake president, the Church called him on April 20, 1935, to serve as managing director of the Church Welfare Program. He received many honors for both his work in the business community and his church service.

To me, however, he showed his true spiritual strength on a cold Sunday morning just a few weeks before his death. President Lee learned of a man hospitalized and critically ill. He immediately went to visit. He gave the man a blessing and then left the room so that the man's wife could have a few tender moments with her husband.

As President Lee walked down the hall, he stopped to put his arm around a young father in a wheelchair holding a lighted cigarette. Two young girls stood by their father. President Lee whispered in the girls' ears, telling them that their father loved them and he knew they loved their father, whether or not he smoked. He then leaned over to the father and spoke words of comfort and encouragement.

During his brief visit, President Lee stopped to speak to a hospital cleaning woman. He shook her hand and thanked her for what she was doing. When the cleaning woman stated she was a Mormon and knew she should be in church, President Lee replied, "Someone has to take care of the sick."

More than all he spoke in sermons and more than all he wrote in books, his example taught how to live. Only weeks before his death, he went to comfort a dying man and his wife, encourage a father addicted to smoking, give hope to the father's little girls, and bless a cleaning woman.

Until his death on December 26, 1973, at the age of seventy-four, President Lee taught by example the Savior's message of service.

Love,

Ritchey Marbury

"It is what you and I give to others that means more than all the sermons we preach."

—HAROLD B. LEE

Hold Fast

Dear Missionaries,

During my early years as a civil engineer and land surveyor, I worked with my father. We often worked on elevated water storage tanks. One day we had the job to inspect an old water tank in Americus, Georgia. After the city drained all the water out of the tank, my father and one other individual climbed inside the tank to inspect it. Dad was probably in his early fifties. The other man was much younger.

Dad started first. The inside ladder had two vertical iron rods and steel bars constructed horizontally between the vertical rods at intervals of about one foot. The horizontal bars were badly corroded and rusted. The vertical climb was more than one hundred feet. It was like climbing into a mist of darkness.

The dark inside of the tank made climbing dangerous, and the rusted horizontal rungs added to the danger. Dad proceeded slowly, holding fast with his left hand to the vertical rod and using his right hand to grasp the horizontal bars. He stepped up with one foot, moved his left hand up, stepped up with his other foot, then moved his right hand up.

"Be careful," Dad shouted to the younger engineer. "Do not climb too quickly and hold fast to the vertical iron rod." The younger engineer, however, paid little attention. He wanted to show how my dad moved too slowly, and how he could do the job much faster.

Dad was probably fifty feet up the ladder when the younger engineer began his climb. By the time Dad reached eighty feet, the younger engineer was at seventy-five feet. Then it happened.

The younger engineer stepped hard on one of the more rusted horizontal bars. It broke. Quickly he clinched his hands around another rung of the ladder. It broke, also. As he fell he kept grabbing the horizontal rungs of the ladder, but every rung gave way. He fell to his death.

The jar from this tragedy caused the horizontal rung that my father was holding to also break. However, he still held fast to the vertical iron rod. It stayed firm and saved his life. My father held fast to the iron rod and lived.

The Book of Mormon records a dream by the prophet Lehi. Numberless concourses of people tried to navigate a narrow path through a mist of darkness. Many wandered off and were lost. Others caught hold of the rod of iron and pressed forward, always clinging to the rod. Those holding fast to the iron rod reached the tree of life and partook of the fruit, and it was good.

The iron rod represents the word of God. The Lord said to Nephi, "Whoso would hearken unto the word of God, and would hold fast unto it, they would never perish; neither could the fiery darts of the adversary overpower them unto blindness, to lead them away to destruction" (I Nephi 15:24).

The iron rod saved my father from physical death as he clung to it. Holding fast to the word of God, which is the meaning of the iron rod in Lehi's dream, will save us all from spiritual death. We learn the word of God as we read the Book of Mormon, the Bible, the Doctrine and Covenants, the Pearl of Great Price, and the messages of living prophets.

Love,

Ritchey Marbury

"Whoso would hearken unto the word of God, and would hold fast unto it, they would never perish; neither could the fiery darts of the adversary overpower them unto blindness, to lead them away to destruction"

—I Nephi 15:24

HOUSE BY THE SIDE OF THE ROAD

Dear Missionaries,

Sam Walter Foss actually lived in a house by the side of the road, and many who knew him said he was always a friend to man. He wrote this poem about his philosophy of life. We would do well to make it ours, also.

The House By The Side Of The Road

There are hermit souls that live withdrawn
In the peace of their self-content;
There are souls, like stars, that dwell apart,
In a fellowless firmament;
There are pioneer souls that blaze their paths
Where highways never ran—
But let me live by the side of the road
And be a friend to man.

Let me live in a house by the side of the road,
Where the race of men go by—
The men who are good and the men who are bad,
As good and as bad as I.

House By The Side Of The Road

I would not sit in the scorner's seat,
Or hurl the cynic's ban—
Let me live in a house by the side of the road
And be a friend to man.

I see from my house by the side of the road,
By the side of the highway of life,
The men who press with the ardor of hope,
The men who are faint with the strife.
But I turn not away from their smiles nor their tears,
Both parts of an infinite plan—
Let me live in my house by the side of the road
And be a friend to man.

I know there are brook-gladdened meadows ahead
And mountains of wearisome height;
That the road passes on through the long afternoon
And stretches away to the night.
But still I rejoice when the travelers rejoice,
And weep with the strangers that moan,
Nor live in my house by the side of the road
Like a man who dwells alone.

Let me live in my house by the side of the road—
Where the race of men go by.
They are good, they are bad, they are weak, they are strong,
Wise, foolish—so am I;
Then why should I sit in the scorner's seat,
Or hurl the cynic's ban?
Let me live in my house by the side of the road
And be a friend to man.

Love,

Ritchey Marbury

*"Let me live in my house by the side of the road
And be a friend to man."*

—S<small>AM</small> W<small>ALTER</small> F<small>OSS</small>

How Did You Die?

Dear Missionaries,

How you live and how you die determines your destiny. Edmund Vance Cooke wrote this poem.

How Did You Die?

Did you tackle that trouble that came your way
With a resolute heart and cheerful?
Or hide your face from the light of day
With a craven soul and fearful?
Oh, a trouble's a ton, or a trouble's an ounce,
Or a trouble is what you make it,
And it isn't the fact that you're hurt that counts,
But only how did you take it?

You are beaten to earth? Well, well, what's that?
Come up with a smiling face.
It's nothing against you to fall down flat,
But to lie there—that's disgrace.
The harder you're thrown, why the higher you bounce;
Be proud of your blackened eye!

It isn't the fact that you're licked that counts,
It's how did you fight—and why?
And though you be done to the death, what then?
If you battled the best you could,
If you played your part in the world of men,
Why, the Critic will call it good.
Death comes with a crawl, or comes with a pounce,
And whether he's slow or spry,
It isn't the fact that you're dead that counts,
But only how did you die?

Love,

Ritchey Marbury

---

*"It's nothing against you to fall down flat,
But to lie there—that's disgrace."*

Edmund Vance Cooke

How To Improve Ability To Teach

Dear Missionaries,

You are all teachers. Full-time missionaries teach the formal discussions, often in the homes of investigators. All members teach, however, just sometimes in less formal settings. You teach by the way that you dress. You teach by the words you use. You teach by what you do at work, home, or play.

The Lord said, "That the thing that will be of most worth unto you will be to declare repentance unto this people, that you may bring souls unto me, that you may rest with them in the kingdom of my Father" (Doctrine and Covenants 15:6. Also Doctrine and Covenants 16:6).

Here are three ways to improve your teaching ability:

1. Study. Doctrine and Covenants 11:21 reads, "Seek not to declare my word, but first seek to obtain my word, and then shall your tongue be loosed; then, if you desire, you shall have my Spirit and my word, yea, the power of God unto the convincing of men."

    Know the gospel so well that you can teach it in a way even children will understand. Harold B. Lee taught that you should also teach so well that no one can misunderstand. Ask questions as you teach, but not questions that intimidate. Too many questions seem like an interrogation.

2. Listen. Ask what is most important to your friends, and don't interrupt while they answer. Listen to understand rather than to reply. When you listen only to reply, you miss opportunities to help. Never show disrespect for another's religion or beliefs. Your goal is to help others have spiritual experiences and to resolve their concerns.

   As you listen to understand, you are better able to help others resolve their concerns. Many people's concerns are like icebergs: only a small portion is visible above the surface. Listen that you may discern needs. Often concerns are more social than doctrinal.

3. Help. Help others have spiritual experiences. Help them gain their own testimonies as you bear yours to them. Help them pray by praying with them. Help them love the scriptures by reading the scriptures with them.

   Gordon B. Hinckley taught that all need friends, responsibilities, and to be nourished by the good word of God. Help those you teach understand that the Church offers all three.

A friend of mine many years ago worked on a survey crew. One day, while the crew worked outside in temperatures above one hundred degrees, tempers flared. No one later even remembered why. Angry words grew into threats. Two of the men decided to settle the issue with fists. My friend stepped between them.

"This is not the way we should act," he said. "Please kneel with me while I pray for calm and understanding." The atmosphere calmed, and the survey crew went back to work. In my more than forty years working as a civil engineer and land surveyor, I have never seen this happen but once. Perhaps it should happen more.

To help others have spiritual experiences, there is one thing you must always do: be nice. That is really the essence of the gospel: be nice. Others sometimes listen to your words, but they always watch your example. Lead by inspiration. Teach by example. Motivate by enthusiasm. Bless by love.

Love,

Ritchey Marbury

"To educate a man in mind and not in morals is to educate a menace to society."

—THEODORE ROOSEVELT

Humility Is A Virtue

Dear Missionaries,

Humility is a virtue. *Webster's Dictionary* defines humility as not being proud or haughty, as being unpretentious. The book *Preach My Gospel* tells us that "humility is willingness to submit to the will of the Lord and to give the Lord the honor for what is accomplished. It includes gratitude for His blessings and acknowledgment of your constant need for His divine help. Humility is not a sign of weakness. It is a sign of spiritual strength."

Our prophets tell us that "to be humble is to recognize gratefully our dependence on the Lord—to understand that we have constant need for His support. Humility is an acknowledgment that our talents and abilities are gifts from God. It is not a sign of weakness, timidity or fear; it is an indication that one knows where their true strength lies. One can be both humble and fearless. One can be both humble and courageous."

Others define humility as teachable. We grow as we learn, and our Heavenly Father is the greatest teacher. Through His Son, Jesus Christ, we learn to love, serve, and sacrifice.

Our leaders also teach us that the opposite of humility is pride, which is condemned in the scriptures. To be prideful is to put greater trust in yourself than in God or in His servants. It is to put the things of the world above the things of God.

Prideful people take honor to themselves. Pride is competitive. Sometimes competition is good, but those who are prideful presume they are better than others. Pride usually results in feelings of anger and hatred, and it is a great stumbling block. It is impossible to be filled with pride when our hearts are filled with charity.

Christ was the perfect example of humility. While suffering in the Garden of Gethsemane, He asked, "O my Father, if it be possible, let this cup pass from me; nevertheless not as I will, but as thou wilt" (Matthew 26:39).

We develop humility as we remember that Heavenly Father is the source of all knowledge, power, and truth. As we do His will, we gain eternal blessings. As we learn to recognize our need to rely on a source greater than ourselves, we gain strength to overcome even the most difficult obstacles. James 4:10 teaches us, "Humble yourselves in the sight of the Lord, and he shall lift you up." This is true.

Love,

Ritchey Marbury

"And whosoever shall exalt himself shall be abased; and he that shall humble himself shall be exalted."

—MATTHEW 23:12

I Can

Dear Missionaries,

"I can do all things through Christ which strengtheneth me" (Philippians 4:13).

Many years ago my wife, Fonda, placed a small can on the podium as she began her talk. On the front of the can was a picture of an eye. She called it her "Eye Can."

We accomplish more focusing on "I can" than "I can't."

I CAN begin each day thanking Heavenly Father for the gift of His Son and the promise of eternal life.

I CAN greet everyone I meet with a smile and a kind word.

I CAN express thanks for any act of kindness by others to me.

I CAN study and prepare myself for opportunities that may come.

I CAN choose never to give up on any worthwhile endeavor, for I know that persistence brings success.

I CAN exercise daily, eat healthy, and avoid harmful substances.

I CAN be a little better today than I was yesterday.

I CAN praise more, criticize less, and look for the good. Doing so will make me a happier person.

I CAN remember that I am a Child of God and as such have the potential for greatness.

I Can

I CAN be a little kinder, laugh more, frown less, give more, and complain less. My potential is limitless, for I am a Child of God.

Love,

Ritchey Marbury

"I can do all things through Christ which strengtheneth me."

—Philippians 4:13

I Went To See My Dentist

Dear Missionaries,

Sometimes what we think will be unpleasant is not so bad after all. Here is a little poem I wrote shortly after I went to see my dentist.

I Went To See My Dentist

I went to see my dentist yesterday.
I must admit it scared me just to think
Of how much it would hurt and what I'd pay
To hear that drill and hear his work tools clink.

He stuffed my mouth with cotton swabs and then
He asked if I was comfortable, and well,
Of course I couldn't talk, just simply grin
And hope I wouldn't jump or scream or yell.

He stuck some pointed tools between my lips.
He scraped my teeth and poked around my gums.
His tools all had bright shiny pointed tips.
His drill made grinding, high-pitched, scary hums.

I Went To See My Dentist

When done, he said I was completely fit.
And I said,' Wow, it didn't hurt a bit!'"

Love,

Ritchey Marbury

"You don't have to look for trouble; it will find you soon enough; and if you don't look for it, it may not find you."

—Ritchey Marbury

In God We Trust

Dear Missionaries,

"And we know that all things work together for good to them that love God" (Romans 8:38). Although you may not recognize it, you see this truth every time you sing the national anthem of the United States of America. Although Francis Scott Key wrote the words to the national anthem as a patriotic hymn during America's battle with England in 1812, the original music was to the tune of an English drinking song.

Under a flag of truce, Francis Scott Key boarded a British flagship in Boston Harbor in order to obtain the release of his friend, Dr. William Beanes. Dr. Beanes was a British prisoner. Since the British fleet was preparing to attack Fort McHenry that day, he and his friend were detained.

They watched the attack all through the night. At dawn the American flag still waved. Francis Scott Key immediately started writing "The Star Spangled Banner." The words came easily, but they worked with the tune of an old English drinking song, "Anacreon in Heaven."

This was the tune he felt impressed to use, but not the same words. John Stafford Smith wrote the original tune as a drinking song for the Anacreontic Society, a London club of the day. Ralph Tomlinson wrote the words, which were:

In God We Trust

> *To Anacreon in Heaven, where he sat in full glee,*
> *A few sons of harmony sent a petition*
> *That he their inspirer and patron would be,*
> *When their answer arrived from the jolly old Grecian:*
> *Voice, fiddle, and flute no longer be mute;*
> *I'll lend ye my name, and inspire ye to boot.*
> *And besides, I'll instruct you, like me, to entwine*
> *The myrtle of Venus with Bacchus's vine.*

Francis Scott Key loved the tune, but not the words. He was a patriot, but also a man with strong religious values. He wanted his words to reflect those values. Most of us know the words to the first verse, but the last verse is less familiar. Here they are:

> *Oh thus be it ever, when free men shall stand*
> *Between their loved homes and the war's desolation!*
> *Blest with victory and peace, may the heav'n-rescued land*
> *Praise the Pow'r that hath made and preserved us a nation!*
> *Then conquer we must, when our cause it is just,*
> *And this be our motto: "In God is our trust!"*
> *And the star spangled banner in triumph shall wave*
> *O'er the land of the free and the home of the brave!*

A tune that once stood for wine and merriment is now best known for patriotism and trust in God.

Love,

Ritchey Marbury

"All things work together for good to them that love God."

—Romans 8:38

It Can Be Done

Dear Missionaries,

Many poets write about the difference between those who say it can't be done and those who say it can. This one is by an unknown author, but the message is the same.

> The man who misses all the fun
> Is he who says "it can't be done."
> In solemn pride he stands aloof
> And greets each venture with reproof.
> Had he the power he'd efface
> The history of the human race;
> We'd have no radio or motor cars,
> No streets lit by electric stars
> No telegraph nor telephone,
> We'd linger in the age of stone.
> The world would sleep if things were run
> By men who say, "It can't be done."

Love,

Ritchey Marbury

> *"The world would sleep if things were run*
> *By men who say, 'It can't be done.'"*
>
> —Author Unknown

Jest 'Fore Christmas

Dear Missionaries,

When I was a child, I looked forward to every Christmas. I knew that day we celebrated the birth of our Savior, Jesus Christ, but I still enjoyed Santa Claus and all the treats and presents. I knew, and still know, the importance of always doing what is right. My parents reminded me just before Christmas, however, that Santa only brought gifts to good little girls and boys. So just before Christmas, I made sure I was as good as I could be; and I still enjoy this poem, "Jest 'Fore Christmas," by Eugene Field.

Jest 'Fore Christmas

Father calls me William, sister calls me Will,
Mother calls me Willie, but the fellers call me Bill!
Mighty glad I ain't a girl—ruther be a boy,
Without them sashes, curls, an' things
that's worn by Fauntleroy!
Love to chawnk green apples an' go swimmin' in the lake—
Hate to take the castor-ile they give for bellyache!

Jest 'Fore Christmas

'Most all the time, the whole year
round, there ain't no flies on me,
But jest 'fore Christmas I'm as good as I kin be!
Got a yeller dog named Sport, sick him on the cat;
First thing she knows she doesn't know where she is at!
Got a clipper sled, an' when us kids goes out to slide,
'Long comes the grocery cart, an' we all hook a ride!
But sometimes when the grocery
man is worrited an' cross,
He reaches at us with his whip, an' larrups up his hoss,
An' then I laff an' holler, "Oh, ye never teched me!"
But jest 'fore Christmas I'm as good as I kin be!

Gran'ma says she hopes that when I git to be a man,
I'll be a missionarer like her oldest brother, Dan,
As was et up by the cannibuls
that lives in Ceylon's Isle,
Where every prospeck pleases, an' only man is vile!
But gran'ma she has never been to
see a Wild West show,
Nor read the Life of Daniel Boone,
or else I guess she'd know
That Buff'lo Bill an' cowboys is good enough for me!
Excep' jest 'fore Christmas, when I'm good as I kin be!

And then old Sport he hangs around,
so solemnlike an' still,
His eyes they seem a-sayin': "What's
the matter, little Bill?"
The old cat sneaks down off her perch
an' wonders what's become
Of them two enemies of hern that
used to make things hum!
But I am so perlite an' tend so earnestly to biz,
That mother says to father: "How
improved our Willie is!"

But father, havin' been a boy hisself, suspicions me
When, jest 'fore Christmas, I'm as good as I kin be!

  For Christmas, with its lots an' lots
   of candies, cakes, an' toys,
  Was made, they say, for proper kids
   an' not for naughty boys;
  So wash yer face an' bresh yer hair,
   an' mind yer p's and q's,
  An' don't bust out yer pantaloons,
   and don't wear out yer shoes;
Say "Yessum" to the ladies, and "Yessur" to the men,
  An' when they's company, don't
   pass yer plate for pie again;
  But, thinkin' of the things yer'd
   like to see upon that tree,
Jest 'fore Christmas be as good as yer kin be!

Love,

Ritchey Marbury

> "But, thinkin' of the things yer'd like to see upon that tree,
> Jest 'fore Christmas be as good as yer kin be!"
>
> —EUGENE FIELD

JOSEPH SMITH TESTIFIES OF JESUS CHRIST

Dear Missionaries,

"And we talk of Christ, we rejoice in Christ, we preach of Christ, we prophesy of Christ, and we write according to our prophecies, that our children may know to what source they may look for a remission of their sins" (2 Nephi 25:26).

Jesus Christ is the head of the Church. He is our leader. He is the one Joseph Smith taught we should follow and obey always.

Joseph Smith taught, "The fundamental principles of our religion are the testimony of the Apostles and Prophets, concerning Jesus Christ, that He died, was buried, and rose again the third day, and ascended into heaven; and all other things which pertain to our religion are only appendages to it" (Documented History of the Church 3:28–30).

Joseph taught that although Jesus was perfect, He was baptized to fulfill all righteousness. Jesus was the only perfect person, yet He suffered much that we would not have to suffer. Jesus healed the sick, made the blind to see, and forgave sin. Joseph taught that Jesus willingly gave His life that we might live forever. No one took His life from Him. No one could, since He was immortal. He gave it willingly.

Joseph taught that Christ rose from the grave on the third day, forever overcoming death. All will live forever, but not all will live with Jesus Christ and Heavenly Father. That is reserved for those who repent of their sins, keep Christ's commandments, and endure to the end.

Joseph taught that through the atonement of Christ, all mankind may be saved by obedience to the laws and ordinances of the gospel.

Joseph taught that Christ would come again, a second time, at the beginning of the millennium. He will reign personally on the earth, and the earth will be renewed and receive its paradisiacal glory.

Joseph taught that the Bible is the word of God as far as it is translated correctly. He taught that the Book of Mormon is a second witness for Jesus Christ and tells of Christ's dealings with the people on the American continent, just as the Bible tells of Christ's teaching to those in and around Jerusalem.

Joseph taught that Heavenly Father, Jesus Christ, and the Holy Ghost are three separate and distinct beings. They are one in purpose. Heavenly Father is the father of our spirits. He loves us all and wants us all to live so that we can return and live with Him. We pray to Heavenly Father in the name of Jesus Christ. Jesus Christ is our Savior. Were it not for Him, none of us could be saved. The Holy Ghost is a comforter and a revealer of truth. The Holy Ghost is the convincing power of God unto us of the truth of the gospel.

Joseph Smith testified of the divinity of our Savior, Jesus Christ, and sealed that testimony in blood with his life.

Love,

Ritchey Marbury

"We believe in God the Eternal Father, and in His Son, Jesus Christ, and in the Holy Ghost."

—First Article of Faith of the Church of Jesus Christ of Latter-day Saints

Joseph Smith Memorial

Just Call Me

Dear Missionaries,

I visited one of my home teaching families the other day. They seemed to be doing well. They certainly did not complain about anything during the visit. They thanked me for coming, and I left with these words, "Just call me if you need anything."

As I left, I thought about a friend from long ago. He also had families to home teach. On one occasion, he brought one of his families a cake. Another time he mowed a family's lawn. Another time he slipped a twenty-dollar bill into a young boy's hand as he left for his first date. "Buy your date some candy or some flowers," he said.

I thought again about my words to my home teaching family. "Just call me" may have satisfied my conscience but did little to help the family.

I have seen families in need and asked the question, "How can I help?" I was always sincere, but perhaps that question did little more than shift the burden from me to those already burdened to the limit.

I plan to continue asking, "How can I help?" and encouraging families, "Just call me if you need anything." I want them to know I am available, but from now on, I plan to do more.

Perhaps we all can do more. We can look for needs and work to meet those needs, even if no one asks. We can bake a cake, mow a lawn, or write a letter. We can visit those in hospitals and nursing homes. We can offer to drive those without transportation to grocery stores or church. We can smile more, complain less, and give more praise.

The words "just call me" are important and good to use as we let others know of our willingness to help. Even better are the words "I see you need help. I'll take care of it right now."

Love,

Ritchey Marbury

"We can't do everything for everyone everywhere, but we can do something for someone somewhere."

—RICHARD L. EVANS

Keep A-Goin'

Dear Missionaries,

When life seems hard, when you feel like quitting, don't. Just keep a-going. Consider this poem by Frank L Stanton.

Keep A-Goin'

If you strike a thorn or rose,
　　Keep a-goin'!
If it hails or if it snows,
　　Keep a-goin'!
'Taint no use to sit an' whine
When the fish ain't on your line;
Bait your hook an' keep a-tryin'—
　　Keep a-goin'!

When the weather kills your crop,
　　Keep a-goin'!
Though 'tis work to reach the top,
　　Keep a-goin'!
S'pose you're out o' ev'ry dime,

Gittin' broke ain't any crime;
Tell the world you're feelin' prime—
    Keep a-goin'!

When it looks like all is up,
    Keep a-goin'!
Drain the sweetness from the cup,
    Keep a-goin'!
See the wild birds on the wing,
Hear the bells that sweetly ring,
When you feel like singin', sing—
    Keep a-goin'!

Love,

Ritchey Marbury

"Though 'tis work to reach the top,
Keep a-goin'!"

—Frank L. Stanton

Keep Pecking Away

Dear Missionaries,

Coleman Cox said, "Even the woodpecker owes his success to the fact that he uses his head and keeps pecking away until he finishes the job he starts." Woodpeckers can peck twenty times per second and tap an estimated eight to twelve thousand times a day.

Success requires persistence. It requires using your head. I don't mean by this that you should go about your day pounding your head over and over again against a wall. I do mean that all of us succeed when we persist in doing what we know to be right, and when we continue doing the right things on a regular basis.

Raw materials develop into life-saving tools when men and women persist in finding ways to use them. Individual notes become hymns and musical masterpieces when composers persist in finding just the right combination. Electricity was always in the clouds, but its value comes only when harnessed in ways that provide power.

Jesus Christ restored His gospel in these latter days, and the entire world deserves the opportunity to hear His message. We have the opportunity to bear testimony to His message. Those of us blessed with the knowledge of truth may find even more blessings as we persist in sharing these truths by our testimony and our actions.

Love,

Ritchey Marbury

"Even the woodpecker owes his success to the fact that he uses his head and keeps pecking away until he finishes the job he starts."

—COLEMAN COX

Last House On The Street

Dear Missionaries,

Every missionary seems to have a story about knocking on the last door or visiting the last house on the street. Elders Roscoe Raymond and Dee Young are no exceptions. I was branch president in Albany, Georgia, at the time.

Thursday evening, August 30, 1973, Elders Raymond and Young told me they met a young man just before lunch that day. They had been going down Edgerly Avenue knocking on every door with no success. They visited every house on the north side of the street and then crossed over to the south side. It was lunchtime. Only a few houses remained. They considered stopping for lunch but decided to continue to the end of the street before stopping.

A young man sat in a rocking chair under a tree as they approached the last house. His name was Steve Hall. Steve told the missionaries he had hoped they would stop to visit with him. The missionaries asked Steve if he would like to know more about Jesus Christ. He answered yes.

The next day, Friday, the missionaries gave Steve some pamphlets and invited him to church. Saturday, Steve rode his brother's bicycle to the missionaries' apartment, where they taught him the first two discussions. Sunday, Steve went to church. That was where I met him for the first time.

Monday, Steve again rode his brother's bicycle to the missionaries' apartment, where they taught him two more discussions. He rode his bicycle to the apartment Tuesday and received two more discussions.

Elder Dee Young baptized Steve at sunrise the next morning, Wednesday, September 5, 1973. He baptized Steve in the Kinchafoonee Creek, just outside of Leesburg, Georgia, and a few miles from the Church. The early morning seminary class for that day was Steve's baptism. The seminary class even sang at his baptism.

Steve had no job when he was baptized, and Ray Jensen, the district president, offered him a job in Tifton, Georgia. Steve worked there about fifteen months before the Church called him to serve as a full-time missionary in the Washington Seattle Mission. His life since his baptism has been one of joys and trials, as with all those who seek to follow the Savior. Since his mission he has served in many callings. One that enriched my life was when he served as my bishop. Steve Hall blessed my life as well as the lives of many others. I'm glad the missionaries listened to the promptings of the spirit and visited that last house.

Love,

Ritchey Marbury

"The secret of success is constancy of purpose."

—BENJAMIN DISRAELI

LEAKY ROOF

Dear Missionaries,

About 4:55 on the afternoon of July 8, 2015, Brandon McGirt drove into his driveway. The dark clouds and the thunder and lightning warned of impending rain. Roofers, anxious to complete the roof on Brandon's house, continued to nail shingles over the roof. They were two hours away from completion. Tarps were available to cover the roof, but the roofers chose to take the risk and keep nailing shingles. Thunder and lightning continued. Still the roofers failed to protect the roof with tarp, hoping to complete their job.

At five fifteen the rains came. As Brandon walked through his bedroom, it seemed as if someone had turned on an overhead sprinkler. First a few drops of water hit his head. He looked up. More water hit his face. Water poured from his roof into the bedroom, kitchen, bathroom, and throughout his house. Brandon called Jana, his wife, to warn her what to expect. Jana was away with a friend but would be home soon.

When Jana arrived home, water covered the floors, furniture, beds, and just about everything in the house. Because the roofers failed to heed the warnings and failed to cover the roof with tarp, rain ruined much of the inside of the house. This letter is not about the failure of the roofers, however. It is about what happened next.

About eight that evening, Jana and Brandon realized they needed help. Jana called their home teacher and the relief society president. Both contacted others. By eight twenty, the home teacher arrived with Elders Schlaich and Rodriguez, two of the full-time missionaries in the area. By eight thirty several others arrived, and by eight forty-five more than ten volunteers were cleaning and moving furniture.

Men and youth carried mattresses outside; others carried furniture. Ladies took loads of clothes and towels home to wash. Several families offered their homes to the McGirt family for as long as they needed a place to stay. The relief society offered food. Whatever the McGirt family needed, someone offered.

Emergencies often bring out the best in people, but people also help others every day. A neighbor brings a friend a sack of tomatoes. A stranger stops to help a stranded motorist fix a flat tire. A child helps carry groceries into the house. A wife prepares a special meal for the family, and a father works two jobs to earn needed income.

A friend sent me a letter the other day for no reason other than to say he was thinking about me. Another friend called my wife to say she was praying for our family. Our children and grandchildren call often just to talk. We live in a wonderful world, and kindness is everywhere.

Johnny lived in Utah and was a member of the Pioneer Stake. He needed a job, but he was mentally retarded and could find no job in industry. Bishop Drury, then storehouse keeper on Welfare Square, gave him a job in the storehouse. Johnny stocked shelves, sorted and packaged potatoes, and worked conscientiously in the storehouse and warehouse.

Johnny worked about forty years at Welfare Square. His hair turned gray with age, but his smile never changed. He always encouraged the other workers and visitors. He served every day simply by being cheerful. He loved the Lord. The Lord loved him, and so did everyone he met. He gave service both in emergencies and every day. That is what missionaries do—just give service.

"And behold, I tell you these things that ye may learn wisdom; that ye may learn that when you are in the service of your fellow beings ye are only in the service of your God" (Mosiah 2:17).

Love,

Ritchey Marbury

"Prayer is good, but when baked potatoes and pudding and milk are needed, prayer will not supply their place on this occasion. Give every duty its proper time and place."

—Brigham Young

Lessons From My Father

Dear Missionaries,

Every Father's Day I think about the first verse in the Book of 1 Nephi. "I Nephi, having been born of goodly parents, therefore I was taught somewhat in all the learning of my father" (1 Nephi 1:1). My father died more than twenty years ago, and I still miss him. He set an example for me that I hope I can come close to following with my own children. Like every earthly father, he wasn't perfect, but he loved me and taught me things that help me every day.

My father loved my mother. I don't believe a father can give a child any greater gift. He held her hand and told her that he loved her every day. Often he brought her a present on Sunday just to show his love. He was always faithful to her. When she was happy, he was happy. He was sad when she was sad. Whenever my mother was sick, or tired, or discouraged, he was there to comfort, uplift, and encourage. He seemed always to know just what my mother needed and did everything in his power to meet those needs.

My father had courage. When his brother was missing in action during World War II, he volunteered to go to war in an effort to find his brother. I remember when the building next to his office caught fire, he rushed into the burning building to save the life of another man trapped inside. When he thought his family was threatened by some criminals, he found they were in Florida, and went to Florida alone to face the men and see that they caused no harm to his family.

My father was a motivator. He was positive in the most negative circumstances. When medical bills depleted our savings, he quietly paid the bills, worked longer hours, and commented, "It was only money." He taught me that "can't" was false doctrine, and we could do anything if we relied on our Heavenly Father and never gave up.

My father gave service. Once a competitor suffered a heart attack and was in the hospital for several weeks. My father got a list of all his competitor's projects and completed them with his own crews and money. He never told his competitor's clients that he did the work, and he gave all the income from that work to his competitor. He always gave 10 percent of his income to charity and taught me to do the same. He gave his best effort on all projects whether or not they were profitable.

My father, along with my mother, taught me to pray. He taught me to trust in Jesus Christ, and that doing what is right is always the right thing to do. He lived what he taught. He attended church regularly and took me with him. He spent time with me—taking me boating, fishing, water skiing, flying airplanes, and working together. He encouraged me to do the same with my children.

Our earthly fathers teach us much about the love our Heavenly Father has for us. My father certainly did. I'm grateful for the years I had with him.

Love,

Ritchey Marbury

"Having been born of goodly parents, therefore I was taught somewhat in all the learning of my father."

—1 Nephi 1:1

Lessons From My Mother

Dear Missionaries,

What I remember most about my mother is that she loved me. No matter what I did, no matter how many mistakes I made, she loved me. I remember sitting on her lap as a young boy as she sang to me and hugged me. She didn't have any special talent for singing, but to me she sounded like an angel. She washed my clothes, cooked my meals, and remembered every special day in my life. She nursed me when I was sick and played games with me when I was lonesome. She prayed for me every day. She taught me the importance of love.

My mother read to me. She read Bible stories, she read nursery rhymes, and she taught me the importance of reading. By the time I started school, I knew most of the Old Testament Bible stories and practically all of the parables of Jesus, because my mother read them to me. I could also quote most of the Mother Goose nursery rhymes.

My mother taught me to enjoy life. She never smoked or drank alcohol, but she could have fun at any party while staying sober and wholesome. She was sick much of her life, but still stayed positive. Weeks before she died, she called a friend to her bedside and asked him if he would make a promise to a dying woman. The man drank too much and was not always faithful to his wife.

Not knowing what Mother would ask, the man agreed to do as she requested. Mother then proceeded to get the man to promise never to drink alcohol again and to quit seeing any other woman but his wife. She told him if he did, she would come back to haunt him after she passed away. The man agreed. After he left, Mother told me he would probably never keep his promise, but he would never enjoy those two vices again.

Mother taught me to encourage others. She always said good things about friends, family, and acquaintances. She was comfortable sitting at the head table with the governor of the state and with the president of Georgia Tech, and she did both. On various occasions, she also ate with janitors, house cleaners, and dirty children. When Fonda and I married in 1962, with our consent, she invited several African Americans to the wedding. She taught me to respect all people based on who they were and not on their social position or the color of their skin.

Mother died at a young age, but her influence never died. I remember her smile, her cheerfulness, and her concern for others as if it were yesterday. She taught me much, even though her years were short. I remember her every Mother's Day, and every other day, also.

Love,

Ritchey Marbury

"A mother like ours is more than a memory. She is a Living Presence."

—TEMPLE BAILEY

LIFE IS FOREVER

Dear Missionaries,

I lost a good friend this morning. It's not the first time someone close departed this life before me. Whenever that happens, I reread a sonnet I wrote years ago called "Life is Forever." It helps me remember that life continues forever, but life on this earth is short. I miss my departed friends and family now, but I will see them again.

> It's just a temporary separation.
> We call it death, but really it's a birth
> Into a place far better than this earth,
> A place of joy and peace and exaltation.
> We grieve for those we love when they are gone.
> We wish we had them back with us to stay,
> But still, we know that though there're gone away
> Their happiness and joyfulness have grown.
> Life is forever and it will endure
> Though death appears to some to be the end.
> Death's not the end, of that you can be sure,
> As sure as sun and stars and rain and wind.

*Because of Christ's atonement we will meet
Departed souls that tell of death's defeat.*

Love,

Ritchey Marbury

---

*"Because of Christ's atonement we will meet
Departed souls that tell of death's defeat."*

—R<small>ITCHEY</small> M<small>ARBURY</small>

LIVE OR DIE, IT'S A WIN-WIN

Dear Missionaries,

Wednesday, August 12, 2015, my wife's sister, Carol Ann Creech, went from this life to the next. She died of a massive stroke due to brain cancer. Shortly before her death, she told her children that, live or die, it was "a win-win situation." Either she would be healed and get to stay on earth with us, or cancer would end her life, and she would be with the Lord.

While speaking to His apostles, Jesus said, "Let not your heart be troubled: ye believe in God, believe also in me. In my Father's house are many mansions: if it were not so I would have told you. I go to prepare a place for you. And if I go and prepare a place for you, I will come again, and receive you unto myself; that where I am, there ye may be also" (John 14:1–3).

Carol Ann had a win-win life. She met her future husband, Bill Creech, in the eighth grade in Albany, Georgia. They dated for a few years, married, and remained married for fifty-seven years. Together they raised three children and had seven grandchildren and two great-grandchildren. She loved life, her family, and her friends. She devoted most of her life to making them happy. She always remained positive with no fear of death. Live or die, it was a win-win.

Love,

Ritchey Marbury

"I go to prepare a place for you. And if I go and prepare a place for you, I will come again, and receive you unto myself; that where I am, there ye may be also."

—John 14:1–3

MAKE SOMEONE HAPPY

Dear Missionaries,

Happiness is not something you buy; it is something you give away. You give away happiness through smiles, genuine complements, small sacrifices, and so many other tender acts. And when you give it away, it comes back.

Think of the times in your life when you were really happy. Were you alone, or were others sharing the happiness with you? Probably you were sharing with others, and some of your happiest moments probably came from your conscious efforts to make someone happy. Happiness is one of those unusual phenomena that seem to elude us when we seek it and find us when we give it away.

Giving away happiness is fun. Try smiling at the next stranger you meet. Give a sincere complement to a working companion or member of your family. Pick out some individual who is frowning or angry and offer to help him or her in some unusual way. Then observe what happens. Life will be richer, if only for a moment.

Making others happy also has tangible rewards, although that's not what you should seek. An airline flight attendant once treated a passenger with such courtesy that the passenger wrote the airline complementing her service. The airline rewarded the courtesy with a free flight to a future destination.

When someone makes you happy, let them know it. That's one way you can share the gift with the giver—and that's what life is all about.

Love,

Ritchey Marbury

"Grief can take care of itself; but to get the full value of joy, you must have somebody to share it with."

—MARK TWAIN

Manner Of Happiness

Dear Missionaries,

The other day I was reading 2 Nephi 5:27. In it Nephi records, "And it came to pass that we lived after the manner of happiness." This seemed a great way to live, but the next verses told little about how to do it. I wanted to live this same way, so I decided to do some research.

Elder Jeffery R. Holland gave a devotional on this subject at Brigham Young University-Idaho on September 23, 2014. He stated that happiness is almost always a by-product of some other endeavor. He then went on to explain what happy people do. He said that, first and foremost, ultimate happiness comes from living the gospel of Jesus Christ.

Second, he taught that happiness is in your hands, not in events or circumstances or fortune or misfortune. He taught that happiness is the consequence of personal effort. He said that he sat in his study for a long time trying to think of any happy person who was unkind or unpleasant. He could think of no one.

Elder Holland also referred to the scripture in 2 Nephi 5:17 where Nephi recorded, "And it came to pass that I, Nephi, did cause my people to be industrious and to labor with their hands." The people of Nephi worked and were a happy people. In contrast, those who failed to follow the teaching of this prophet became idle people, full of mischief and subtlety.

As I continued to think about happiness, I thought to myself, "Just what is happiness?" To me happiness is having family and friends who are close. It is being healthy, being at peace with myself, and knowing I can be with these friends and family forever as I follow the teaching of Christ. It is loving others and being loved by others. As Elder Holland taught, happiness is living the gospel of Jesus Christ.

Love,

Ritchey Marbury

"Ultimate happiness comes from living the gospel of Jesus Christ."

—Jeffery R. Holland

Matthew Cowley's Good Night's Sleep

Dear Missionaries,

Glen L. Rudd tells the story of Matthew Cowley's last days on this earth. Elder Cowley, a member of the Council of the Twelve Apostles, gave his farewell address at the October 1953 general conference. He planned to talk on baptism, but talked on another subject. Totally at ease, he talked about passing away to the other side. Throughout October and November, he told Brother Rudd he didn't believe he would live much longer.

On December 3, Brother Rudd drove Elder Cowley to Logan, Utah, where Elder Cowley participated in a panel discussion at the university. On the return trip, they discussed last-minute things Elder Cowley wanted Brother Rudd to do for him. As they entered Salt Lake City, Elder Cowley said, "Let's not go home. Let's go get a bowl of soup."

The two of them sat in the back booth of a Chinese restaurant for over three hours. Finally, at eleven thirty that evening, the manager asked that they go home so that he could close up. As they left Elder Cowley remarked, "I know I am going to die one of these mornings soon. I'm not going to die until after I have had a good night's sleep. I'm not going to the other side all tired out. When I go to bed at night now, I look around the house, give my wife a little extra kiss, say my prayers, get into bed, and then go to sleep. I know the exact time I will pass away."

"If I knew I was going to die some night, I don't believe I could go to sleep," said Brother Rudd.

"Oh yes you would," said Elder Cowley. "You know as well as I do that life is eternal. If I go to bed and pass away in my sleep, then when I wake up on the other side, I'll do what whoever is in charge of me tells me to do. If I wake up and I'm still here, then I'll do what President McKay tells me to do here, so what difference does it make? Life is eternal."

President McKay was then president of the Church.

After Brother Rudd told how nervous he would be in the same situation, Elder Cowley replied, "Well, if you knew what I knew, you wouldn't be nervous. It's fine with me. I'm happy. I think this is the way it ought to be."

Elder Cowley said he didn't know the exact day he would die, but said to Brother Rudd, "You know what time I wake up every day?

"Yes," said Brother Rudd.

"Well, before I pass away, I'm going to get a good night's sleep, and then at the time I generally wake up, I will take a big deep breath, turn over, and just quietly drift away. There won't be any pain or suffering or any other difficulty, and that's just the way I've always wanted it to be. It's all arranged, and I'm looking forward to it."

That's exactly how he died. He and the Lord, according to Brother Rudd, were able to reach a calm agreement when he would conclude his life's activities. What a great experience for Brother Rudd to live so close to a man who lived so close to the Lord. What a great experience for Fonda and me to know a man such as Brother Rudd, who also lives so close to the Lord.

As Elder Cowley said, "Life is eternal." As missionaries—full time or missionaries by virtue of President McKay's statement that every member is a missionary—we can teach that same truth to others by our testimony, our example, and our faith.

Love,

Ritchey Marbury

"Death, though bitter to observe, is not the end, but is, rather, only another graduation from which we go on to a better life."

—Gordon B. Hinckley

MIGHTY CHANGE OF HEART

Dear Missionaries,

"And now behold, I ask of you, my brethren of the Church, have ye spiritually been born of God? Have ye received his image in your countenances? Have ye experienced this mighty change in your hearts?" (Alma 5:14).

"And now behold, I say unto you, my brethren, if ye have experienced a change of heart, and if ye have felt to sing the song of redeeming love, I would ask, can ye feel so now?" (Alma 5:26)

You feel close to Heavenly Father many times. Alma teaches that you get those feelings when you exercise faith and when your works are the works of righteousness. He teaches that you gain these feelings when you have clean hands and a pure heart. Alma also tells what causes you to lose those feelings.

Alma asks, "Could you say if ye were called to die at this time, within yourselves, that ye have been sufficiently humble?" (Alma 5:27). Humility is being teachable. It is recognizing your need to rely on a power greater than yourself. Lack of humility is like the soldier marching in a parade complaining that everyone, other than he, is out of step. It is like the apprentice who failed to follow the teaching of the master. Although unsuccessful, when asked why he failed to follow the master's advice, he answered, "I found a better way."

Alma warns about pride. He teaches that if you are prideful, you are not prepared to meet God. It is good to do the best you can do, and it is good to care about the quality of your efforts. However, snobbery is foolish pride. It is the trait of one not sure of their position. As stated in Proverbs 16:18, "Pride goeth before destruction, and an haughty spirit before a fall."

Alma asks if you are stripped of envy. Do you delight in the good fortune of others? Are you happy at their success, or do you wish them failure, so that you can succeed instead? Alma warns that if you are envious, you are not prepared to meet God. He warns you to prepare quickly.

Alma asks if there is one among you that doth make a mock of his brother, or that heapeth upon him persecutions. Do you make unkind jokes about those less fortunate? Do you discriminate against those with different clothes, with different skin color, or who are less educated? Woe unto such an one, Alma teaches, for he is not prepared, and the time is at hand that he must repent or he cannot be saved.

"And now, my brethren, I would that ye should hear me, for I speak in the energy of my soul; for behold, I have spoken plainly that ye cannot err, or have spoken according to the commandments of God" (Alma 5:43).

Alma teaches that all must come unto the Savior and bring forth works of righteousness. He teaches how to, once again, feel that mighty change of heart. He teaches how to continue to feel the song of redeeming love.

Love,

Ritchey Marbury

"And now behold, I say unto you, my brethren, if ye have experienced a change of heart, and if ye have felt to sing the song of redeeming love, I would ask, can ye feel so now?"

—ALMA 5:14

Mother's Day Tribute

Dear Missionaries,

Of all God's creations, perhaps mothers are the finest. Not just on Mother's Day, but every day we live, we do well to pay tribute to our mothers. We have them from our first existence on earth. They care for us and protect us from dangers of all description. They sacrifice for us in ways no others could or would.

Harold B. Lee said, "A good mother or wife may render a husband more perfect than he otherwise would be."

When someone asked Elder Russell M. Nelson why he chose to be a doctor, he answered that it was his opinion that the highest and noblest work in this life is that of a mother. Since that option was not available to him, he thought caring for the sick might come close.

Mothers understand priorities. Harold B. Lee told of a mother polishing pieces of silver as she prepared for an evening reception. Her eight-year-old son came by with a piggy bank and asked, "Mother, how do you pay tithing?"

She did not want interruptions, but she stopped to explain. The son thanked her. She then went back to polishing the silver. The interruption may have prevented her from getting all the silver polished before the reception, but she understood what was important.

Commenting later, when asked why she chose to answer her son rather than finish what she was doing she said this, "All my life I will have time to polish silver, but this may be the only time I will ever have to teach my son the principle of tithing."

Homes are largely what mothers make them. Mothers have the ability to tune in to their child's wavelength and pick up the first signs of difficulty, danger, and distress. This ability may save a child from disaster.

Mothers nurture. Mothers love. Mothers care. Mothers understand. Mothers read to their children. Mothers place the child before all else, and in so doing mold the future of the child.

Strickland Gillilan paid tribute to mothers who read to their children by writing this poem. It tells of just one of the blessings of having a good mother.

The Reading Mother

I had a Mother who read to me
Sagas of pirates who scoured the sea,
Cutlasses clenched in their yellow teeth,
"Blackbirds" stowed in the hold beneath.
I had a Mother who read me lays
Of ancient and gallant and golden days;
Stories of Marmion and Ivanhoe,
Which every boy has a right to know.
I had a Mother who read me tales
Of Gelert the hound of the hills of Wales,
True to his trust till his tragic death,
Faithfulness blent with his final breath.
I had a Mother who read me the things
That wholesome life to the boy heart brings—
Stories that stir with an upward touch,
Oh, that each mother of boys were such!
You may have tangible wealth untold;

Caskets of jewels and coffers of gold.
Richer than I you can never be—
I had a Mother who read to me.

Love,

Ritchey Marbury

"Richer than I you can never be—
I had a mother who read to me."

—S𝁂𝁃𝁂𝁄

—STRICKLAND GILLILAN

My Choice

Dear Missionaries,

I read a poem the other day that made me chuckle. It also taught a valuable lesson. The author is unknown. Here it is:

My Choice

> I'd rather be a **Could Be**
> If I could not be an **Are!**
> For a **Could Be** is a **May Be**
> With a chance of making par.
> I'd rather be a **Has Been**
> Than a **Might Have Been** by far,
> For a **Might Have Been** has never been,
> But a **Has Been** was once an **Are!**

Love,

Ritchey Marbury

*"I'd rather be a **Has Been**
Than a **Might Have Been** by far."*

—A<small>NONYMOUS</small>

My Soul Delighteth In Plainness

Dear Missionaries,

I read a report by the government yesterday regarding instructions on how to prevent erosion. The report stated that "best management practices, including sound conservation and engineering practices to prevent and minimize erosion and resultant sedimentation, must be consistent with, and no less stringent than, those practices in the Manual for Erosion and Sediment Control." The report went on to include more than one hundred pages describing best management practices and other required procedures.

After reading the report, I understood part of it but needed to read and reread many pages to understand. I was amazed to see how many words could be used to explain how "fast running water causes erosion." The details in this report were probably necessary, but I appreciate the words of Nephi when he said, "My soul delighteth in plainness" (2 Nephi 31:3).

The Lord's instructions to us are plain and easily understood: Love God. Honor your father and mother. Do not steal. Do not kill. Do not commit adultery. These are a few of the instructions in the Ten Commandments.

If you want a shorter version of the Lord's instructions, He tells us to love God and love our neighbor. Hartman Rector Jr., in one of his talks that I remember most, made it even plainer. He summarized the gospel in just two words: "Be nice."

We all know what the Lord would have us do. The Lord made His instructions clear. "Verily I say, men should be anxiously engaged in a good cause, and do many things of their own free will, and bring to pass much righteousness" (Doctrine and Covenants 58:27). As President Spencer W. Kimball said so many times, just "do it."

Love,

Ritchey Marbury

"Be nice."

—Hartman Rector, Jr.

Nadine Oldham

Dear Missionaries,

Nadine Oldham is remarkable. I home teach her, and she cheers me up on every visit. Last week I visited her, and she invited me to race her along a small sidewalk. She raced in her wheelchair, and she won. A few weeks before, she insisted I go with her to visit some of her friends. She said they needed cheering up and she wanted to be sure someone took care of them.

What is remarkable about Nadine is that she has myasthenia gravis, a neuromuscular disease that confines her to a wheelchair. Her disease is progressing slowly, so that sometimes she is able to stand for only one or two minutes. Other than those one or two minutes, she moves about in her motorized wheelchair. She refuses to let physical limitations slow her.

She lives in an assisted-living home and tells me she loves it there. She spends her days visiting patients in adjoining rooms, doing her best to make them feel happy and cheerful. She says the nurses sometimes get depressed because of the condition of the patients. When that happens, she cheers them up by inviting them to race her down the hall—she in her wheelchair and they running beside her. Sometimes they get in trouble while racing, but she loves it.

Some say that happiness is a state of mind and you can be happy if you just make up your mind to be so. Nadine is a great example of this. She spends her time making others happy, and in so doing makes herself happy. According to 2 Corinthians 9:7, "God loveth a cheerful giver." The Lord surely loves Nadine.

Love,

Ritchey Marbury

"Let us be kind to one another, for most of us are fighting a hard battle."

—IAN MACLAREN

Nadine Oldham in Her Wheelchair Racing Ritchey Marbury

NOBILITY

Dear Missionaries,

"True worth is in being, not seeming." With these words Alice Cary begins her poem "Nobility." Her message is worth hearing again and again.

Nobility

True worth is in being, not seeming,
In doing, each day that goes by,
Some little good—not in dreaming
Of great things to do by and by.

For whatever men say in their blindness,
And spite of the fancies of youth,
There's nothing so kingly as kindness,
And nothing so royal as truth.

We get back our meet as we measure—
We cannot do wrong and feel right,
Nor can we give pain and gain pleasure,
For justice avenges each slight.

Nobility

The air for the wing of the sparrow,
The bush for the robin and wren,
But always the path that is narrow
And straight, for the children of men.

'Tis not in the pages of story
The heart of its ills to beguile,
Though he who makes courtship to glory
Gives all that he hath for her smile.

For when from her heights he has won her,
Alas it is only to prove
That nothing's so sacred as honor,
And nothing so loyal as love!

We cannot make bargains for blisses,
Nor catch them like fishes in nets;
And sometimes the thing our life misses
Helps more than the thing which it gets.

For good lieth not in pursuing,
Nor gaining of great nor of small,
But just in the doing, and doing
As we would be done by, is all.

Through envy, through malice, through hating,
Against the world, early and late,
No jot of our courage abating—
Our part is to work and to wait.

And slight is the sting of his trouble
Whose winnings are less than his worth;
For he who is honest is noble,
Whatever his fortunes or birth.

Love,

Ritchey Marbury

*"We get back our meet as we measure—
We cannot do wrong and feel right."*

—A<small>LICE</small> C<small>ARY</small>

Not In Vain

Dear Missionaries,

Sometimes people say a lot in just a few words. This is the case with Emily Dickinson's poem "Not in Vain."

Not In Vain

If I can stop one heart from breaking,
I shall not live in vain:
If I can ease one life the aching,
Or cool one pain,
Or help one fainting robin
Unto his nest again,
I shall not live in vain.

Love,

Ritchey Marbury

*"If I can stop one heart from breaking,
I shall not live in vain."*

—Emily Dickinson

Nothing Shall Be Impossible

Dear Missionaries,

"For verily I say unto you, if ye had the faith as a grain of mustard seed, ye shall say unto this mountain, remove hence to yonder place; and it shall remove; and nothing shall be impossible unto you" (Matthew 17:20).

July 19, 1913, a lad was born. He weighed about two pounds. His mother had carried him in her womb only seven months. He wasn't expected to live, but his parents had faith. When the doctors said he probably would die, they told the doctor not to give up. They said their prayers every morning. They said their prayers every evening. They went to church every Sunday, and Matthew 17:20 says, "Nothing shall be impossible unto you."

The boy lived. He was my father. He grew up working on a farm. He milked cows, drew water from their well, planted, plowed, and tended to small crops. He attended Albany High School in Albany, Georgia. There he learned how to box.

One day a large two-hundred-pound ruffian tried to bully my father. Dad would not back down, and a brawl almost started. It would have except for some school leaders. Dad suggested they settle their differences in the ring—the boxing ring.

The bully also went to Albany High School and was the current golden gloves heavyweight boxing champion. My dad weighed 135 pounds and stood five feet five and three-quarter inches tall.

This was a three-round bout. The champion knocked Dad out of the ring twice in the first round. Twice Dad returned to the ring. The second round the champion knocked Dad out of the ring three times. Three times Dad returned to the ring. The third round the champion again knocked Dad out of the ring. When Dad returned, the champion stared in disbelief.

"It's impossible for someone to be knocked out of the ring so many times and still be able to fight," thought the champion. He dropped his guard for a second. Dad landed a solid right, a solid left, and another solid right. The champion staggered. Two minutes into the three-minute round, the referee declared my dad the winner by a technical knockout. At 135 pounds my dad was now the golden gloves heavyweight champion.

Some said that was impossible. But it wasn't. After all, Dad said his prayers every morning, said his prayers every evening, and went to church every Sunday, and Matthew 17:20 says, "Nothing shall be impossible unto you."

Dad worked on the docks in Florida one summer. Because of his small size, the dock foreman did not want to give Dad the job. He pointed to a one-hundred-pound sack of fertilizer and asked, "Do you think you can carry sacks like that around all day?"

Dad quietly lifted the first sack with one hand and another with the other hand. "Where shall I take these sacks?" he asked.

"That's impossible," said the foreman. "No one your size can lift sacks that heavy."

"You don't understand. I say my prayers every morning. I say my prayers every evening. I go to church every Sunday, and Matthew 17:20 says nothing shall be impossible unto you."

Dad got the job and worked there the entire summer.

Dad continued his boxing career while attending college at Georgia Tech. Many expected him to represent the United States in the Olympics. During the Olympic trials, however, be broke his knuckles during the first round of the bout and failed to win. This was probably a blessing, since had he gone to the Olympics he might have chosen a career in boxing. Instead, he became a professional engineer and registered land surveyor, providing me with the incentive to do the same.

Dad volunteered to serve with the US Navy during World War II. While serving he watched a young man pray, kneeling inside his tent. A burly 230-pound sailor yanked the young man, cursed at him, and said only sissies said prayers. This was war and he wanted no sissies in his camp.

Dad pulled the sailor aside, stating that he prayed also. Just then the navy chaplain stepped up.

"Ordinarily," said the chaplain, "we would settle this in a boxing ring. But considering the difference in size…"

Dad stopped him. "Put us in the ring together. He needs to be taught a lesson."

The chaplain hesitated, then agreed.

It was a short fight. Dad knocked the 230-pound sailor out in the first few minutes of the first round. When the sailor got up, he stared at my dad and said, "That's impossible. I can whip anyone in this camp. How can a little man like you knock me unconscious?"

Dad grinned. "I say my prayers every morning. I say my prayers every evening. I go to church every Sunday. Matthew 17:20 says nothing shall be impossible unto you."

The 230-pounder got up. He had a grin on his face. "Until today I could lick any man in this camp, but I never prayed and I never went to church. This Sunday I expect to see every one of you in church, and if not you will answer to me, and I will be able to lick any one of you. How do I know? I plan to say my prayers every morning. I plan to say my prayers every evening. I plan to go to church every Sunday, and I now know that Matthew 17:20 says nothing shall be impossible unto you."

The men in that camp did attend church faithfully. They fought together in Siapan, Tinian, Iwo Jima, and other islands in the Pacific. Most of them came home safely, including my father.

I'm grateful for a father who taught me to pray morning and evening and who taught me to attend church. He taught by example, and that example motivated me to do the same all my life. He lived eighty years, and from the time I was eleven, we worked together most of his life. He taught me that, as I remember to say my prayers every morning, say my prayers every evening, and go to church every Sunday, as Matthew 17:20 says, "nothing shall be impossible."

Love,

Ritchey Marbury

"Nothing shall be impossible unto you."

—Matthew 17:20

Old Home Place

Dear Missionaries,

Fonda and I have lived in our home on Green Valley Lane in Albany, Georgia, for almost fifty years. Our children have all moved away, as have many of our closest friends. Someday we may have to move, but we have no plans to do so. We love our home, and many of you reading these letters probably have a place you call home. You may still live there, or you may have moved away, but that old home place still brings happy memories of days gone by. I wrote this sonnet about our home.

The Old Home Place

The old home place, where memories abound,
Where sounds of laughter rang with playful glee,
Where once the children played upon the ground
And built a playhouse high up in a tree.

We had a garden almost every year.
We planted peas and beans, tomatoes and some corn.
For holidays we had our loved ones near.
For birthdays we gave thanks for being born.

Old Home Place

I love that old home place; it brought me peace;
It helped bring comfort during times of pain.
The memories of it will never cease.
It sheltered us from cold and wind and rain.

Perhaps another place we'll dwell someday,
But love of that old home is here to stay.

Love,

Ritchey Marbury

"A happy family is but an earlier heaven."

—Sir John Bowring

Only A Dad

Dear Missionaries,

I think of my dad often, as I am sure many of you do. This poem by Edgar Guest reminds me of my dad and the many things he did for me both in my youth and later as I grew older.

Only A Dad

Only a dad with a tired face,
Coming home from the daily race,
Bringing little of gold or fame,
To show how well he has played the game,
But glad in his heart that his own rejoice
To see him come and to hear his voice.

Only a dad with a brood of four,
One of ten million men or more.
Plodding along in the daily strife,
Bearing the whips and the scorns of life,
With never a whimper of pain or hate,
For the sake of those who at home await.

Only A Dad

Only a dad, neither rich nor proud,
Merely one of the surging crowd
Toiling, striving from day to day,
Facing whatever may come his way,
Silent, whenever the harsh condemn,
And bearing it all for the love of them.

Only a dad but he gives his all
To smooth the way for his children small,
Doing, with courage stern and grim,
The deeds that his father did for him.
This is the line that for him I pen:
Only a dad, but the best of men.

Love,

Ritchey Marbury

"Only a dad, but the best of men."

—EDGAR GUEST

Only Doers Fail

Dear Missionaries,

Failure is something we can avoid by doing nothing, saying nothing, and being nothing. I never failed at running a marathon because I never tried. None of us will be successful at everything, but we all can be successful at many things by concerted effort.

Albert Einstein tried and failed often. He tried to speak, but failed until he was four. He tried to read, but was seven before he could. He wanted to go to school, but was expelled and refused admittance to the Zurich Polytechnic School. He failed at math, but eventually won the Nobel Prize for his work as a mathematician and physicist.

Thomas Edison's teachers told him he was "too stupid to learn anything." His employers at his first two jobs fired him. He failed about one thousand times when attempting to invent the light bulb, but he was a doer, and he succeeded.

Abraham Lincoln went to war as a captain and returned as a private. Winston Churchill failed the sixth grade. In his early years, Walt Disney worked for a newspaper. His editor fired him because he "lacked imagination and had no good ideas."

Lucille Ball was once widely regarded as a failed actress and second-tier movie star. Her drama instructors told her she couldn't make it in acting and to try another profession. She failed because she was a doer. She never quit. During her career she had thirteen Emmy nominations and won four. She also earned the Lifetime Achievement Award from the Kennedy Center Honors.

Only doers fail because only doers try. Those that do nothing may not fail, but they also never achieve.

Love,

Ritchey Marbury

"For not the hearers of the law are just before God, but the doers of the law shall be justified."

—Romans 2:13

Pounding On Bent Nails

Dear Missionaries,

Have you ever tried to drive a nail into a board only to have the nail bend before you finished the job? If you have, then you know you have choices. You can yell, scream, and holler, which will do no good. You can continue pounding on the bent nail, only to find it bends it further; or you can pull the nail and pat it on its back. As you gently pat the nail, you may find it straightens and again becomes useful.

People are like nails. They may bend and quit functioning when the pressure is too great. They may yell and scream, but it will do no good. They may simply not have the strength or will to carry on. What they need is not a blow to the head, but a pat on the back.

Most of the time when others act irrational, they are saying, "Help me. I'm overwhelmed and don't know what to do." A pat on the back and a kind word may be all the help needed.

Love,

Ritchey Marbury

"Let us be kind to one another, for most of us are fighting a hard battle."

—Ian Maclaren

Prayer Feeds Missionary

Dear Missionaries,

Prayer works, especially when it is to help a hungry missionary. That was the case in Boise, Idaho, in 1980. In those days missionaries lived on what parents sent, or what the missionary could save before the mission. If the missionary received no money from home, the missionary went without. One missionary in Boise lived on what his mother could send from her work as a church custodian. The amount was so meager that, during some months, he only ate one meal a day.

This was an unusually dedicated missionary. He taught more than fifteen discussions per day and ran from door to door when tracting. He kept every mission rule with exactness as far as I could tell. But he lived on much less than the other missionaries in the mission. His parents just did not have the money to help.

One morning I went into my office alone to pray. I told Heavenly Father how hard this missionary worked and pleaded for financial help. I knew Heavenly Father answered prayers, and I knew that He knew this missionary deserved help. After only a few minutes in prayer, I had a good feeling. I arose to hear the telephone.

A voice on the other end of the phone asked, "Are you the president of the Boise, Idaho, mission?"

"Yes," I replied.

"Well," the voice said, "I don't know why, but I had the strongest urge to stop what I was doing and call the Idaho Boise mission president. Do you have a missionary there that needs help?"

"I sure do," I said. "I just finished a prayer for this missionary asking for financial help so that he would have enough money on his mission to eat well and have sufficient clothing."

"I knew some help was needed. Tell me how to contact this missionary, and I will pay all expenses for the rest of his mission."

This man did exactly as he promised. He paid all expenses for the missionary from that time forth. This missionary baptized more than two hundred converts during his two years of service. He returned to the mission shortly after his release to tell me that there was one person he and I had taught together who was not baptized. He insisted we visit that person again. We did and the person was later baptized.

Sometimes we fail to get the results we desire because we fail to ask. Heavenly Father always answers prayer and always answers it in the way that is best for those who pray and those affected by the prayer. It may not be answered as soon as we wish and in the way we expect. We may not understand why it is answered in the way that it is, but it is always answered in the way that is best. In this case Heavenly Father answered my prayer quickly and wonderfully.

Love,

Ritchey Marbury

"He who has ceased to pray has lost a great friendship."

—Richard L. Evans

Preparation Precedes Performance

Dear Missionaries,

I learned to fly in a single-engine Cessna 150. Gary Cooper (not the actor) was my instructor. He had thousands of hours of flying experience and many successful students. After I completed my first solo, he taught me how to fly in good weather, bad weather, and emergencies. First, he taught me that the best way to be safe is to fly in good weather. Don't tempt the elements.

As I grew more proficient, he taught me how to fly in emergencies. Every lesson, at some point during the flight, he would pull the throttle, eliminating power to the airplane, and would have me find a place to land the airplane and then land it. Sometimes he would even pull the power on takeoff. Power failure on takeoff is the most dangerous time to lose power, and he wanted me to know what to do in case I ever experienced that danger.

Gary also insisted I read the instructor's manual for every airplane I flew and that I study the required material to pass the written exam to get my license. He wasn't satisfied if I knew 80 or even 90 percent of the material. He wanted me to understand 100 percent of everything in the manual. Even after I obtained my pilot's license, he took me up on occasion to practice emergency skills.

His training and insistence that I practice emergency procedures probably saved my life.

Preparation Precedes Performance

One Friday evening I left the Sanford, Florida, airport for Albany, Georgia. A man with whom I was working asked me to fly him to Tallahassee. I agreed. I was flying a rented airplane but felt comfortable flying it since I had flown that type of plane many times before.

We landed in Tallahassee after dark but had no trouble landing since runway lights highlighted the runway. I did notice some small sputtering in the engine but wasn't concerned.

My passenger unloaded, and I took off again for home. Then it happened. Just as I crossed the end of the runway, the engine quit. It was dark. I couldn't see anything other than the instrument panel on my airplane. I knew, somehow, I had to turn the plane around and land back on the runway.

The emergency did not seem real at the time. I had practiced this several dozen times with my instructor. Immediately I set the plane on its maximum glide slope and began executing a 180-degree turn. I radioed the control tower that I had no power and requested they clear the runway for an emergency landing.

The tower operator responded by giving me the weather report.

"I have been flying most of the day," I replied. "I know what the weather is. I will be on the ground somewhere in about ninety seconds, and I hope it is on your runway."

"Cleared to land on any runway," the tower operator responded.

By now I could see the lights in the city, but I still could not see the runway. I looked at the altimeter and my rate of decent. Another forty-five seconds and I would be on the ground somewhere. I looked everywhere for the runway. I still saw nothing. Now I began to realize my predicament. I would be on the ground somewhere in another thirty seconds.

Lights. Runway lights. I was too low to make the 180-degree turn planned but probably could land on the cross runway. Boy was I glad to see those lights on the cross runway. Ten seconds left.

Just as I calculated, I touched down ten seconds later—on the runway. I tried again to start the airplane. It started and I taxied the plane to the hanger. The tower operator radioed to ask if I wanted to take off again and fly the airplane home. I told him that the plane could sit at the airport forever as far as I was concerned. I was renting a car and driving home.

I am probably alive today because of the training and practice required by my instructor. I was prepared when the emergency came, and my response was automatic. There was no thought as to whether I should try to restart the plane in the air, no thought as to what was the proper glide slope, and no thought as to what airspeed I must maintain to keep the plane flying. All was automatic.

Life is like that. We may at times enjoy a leisurely life, where everything is routine. Then the trials and temptations come. They may be subtle or drastic. We respond best when we prepare in advance. It is best to avoid temptations. It is best to stay away from situations where temptations are strong, but often life brings surprises. How we respond to life's surprises could affect our eternal happiness. Our goal should be automatic righteous decisions.

Preparation is the key. Be familiar with your instruction manuals, which are your scriptures. Listen to your instructors, who are the general authorities of the Church. Practice what you learn by reading your scriptures daily, having personal and family prayer daily, and giving service. Think about decisions you may need to make, and make them in advance, when there is ample time to study them out in your mind.

Preparation and following flying instruction saved my mortal life. Preparation and following spiritual instruction will save your eternal life.

Love,

Ritchey Marbury

"But if ye are prepared ye shall not fear."

—DOCTRINE & COVENANTS 38:30

Prepare Or Procrastinate

Dear Missionaries,

Alma gives two warnings to the world: "This life is the time for men to prepare to meet God" (Alma 34:32), and "Do not procrastinate the day of your repentance" (Alma 34:33). He gives more warnings and teaches more truths, but attention to these warnings will give much spiritual safety.

Preparedness brings safety. Most of us have experienced a flat tire during travel. I have. In my younger years, I always had a spare tire and a jack available when traveling by car. Several times my tires went flat, but this presented few problems. Within a few minutes, I could change the tire and be back on my journey.

Several months ago I had another flat tire. This time I was not prepared. I did have a spare tire, but no jack. Not only that, but the spare tire was impossible to reach without special tools, which I also did not have. Luckily, I did have a cell phone and called for help—which arrived about an hour later. My failure to prepare for such emergency caused much anxiety and frustration.

Thunderstorms are common where I live in South Georgia. Many times during these storms, my home loses power for several hours. If the storms occur at night, I have light only if I am prepared with flashlights, candles, or other forms of emergency light. Computer failure is also common, and unless my data is backed up by some acceptable method, the data is lost and recovery difficult if not impossible.

My wife lost her sister a few weeks ago. Feeling the need to see her before she passed, we dropped our other plans and drove the five hours to her home. She died a few weeks later. We thank our Heavenly Father often that He prompted us not to procrastinate that visit.

As important as being prepared for life's emergencies is, preparation for eternal salvation is even more important. We prepare to meet God by prayer, scripture study, and giving service. We will make mistakes, so repentance is necessary. We repent by confessing and forsaking our mistakes, and striving to live more Christlike lives in the future. We make restitution where possible.

President Spencer W. Kimball once said that he could never be in too much trouble with Heavenly Father because he repented so often. If a prophet of God felt the need to repent often, all of us should take heed not to procrastinate our repentance.

Alma also taught, "If ye have procrastinated the day of your repentance even until death, behold, ye have become subjected to the spirit of the devil, and he doth seal you his" (Alma 34:35). Perhaps there will be some opportunities to accept the gospel and repent in the spirit world, but do we really want to take that chance?

Love,

Ritchey Marbury

"Do not procrastinate the day of your repentance."

—Alma 34:33

RED KNOT SUCCESS HABITS

Dear Missionaries,

You don't have to be the best, the strongest, or the largest to succeed. You just have to develop the right habits. Persistence, endurance, planning, and flexibility are success habits red knots teach us.

Red knots are shorebirds only two-thirds the size of a pigeon, measuring only about ten inches from bill to tail. They weigh about six ounces.

Red knots sometimes fly nonstop for six days and nights from southern Brazil to North Carolina, a distance of almost five thousand miles. These same shorebirds, on other occasions, fly nonstop for eight days and more than three thousand miles from Canada's Hudson Bay to the Caribbean. In one year some red knots cover 16,600 miles during migratory flights from their Artic breeding grounds to their South American wintering grounds, one of the longest recorded annual distances flown by any known species of bird.

Red knots breed in the high Artic during the months of June through August. Days are long during those months and insects supplying food are plentiful. They mate, they build their nests on high dry ground, and the females lay four camouflaged eggs in about six days. The eggs weigh more than half the female's own body weight. After they help care for their young during the first few days of life, females leave and migrate south to Florida or South America. Males stay behind to continue care until the young are able to care for themselves; then they leave. Juvenile red knots begin their own migration two or three weeks after the adults leave.

In March and April, red knots migrate from their winter homes, as far south as Tierra del Fuego in South America, to their breeding grounds in the Artic. Their flight of six to ten thousand miles often includes a stop along the Atlantic Coast. Delaware Bay is one of the most popular. There the shorebirds feast on horseshoe crab eggs, blue mussels, worms, and other invertebrates for about two weeks. They double their bodyweight before resuming flight to their Artic breeding grounds, and the cycle repeats itself.

Red knots persist and endure. They achieve success at feats not even attempted by larger and stronger birds. Although they weigh only six ounces and are less than a foot long, they navigate thousands of miles to reach their desired destination. They do not give up because they are small and often hungry. Size does not determine their success. They persist. They endure, and they succeed.

Red knots plan. While flying more than sixteen thousand round-trip miles in a year, they have a regular plan for refueling. During their breeding flights, they have planned stops along the Atlantic Coast, where they feed for about two weeks before continuing their journey. They have similar stops when returning south for the winter. The stops are all in areas where known food exists, or has existed in the past.

Red knots are flexible. They know how to deal with emergencies, sometimes making extensive detours around tropical storms during migrations. If one route doesn't work, they find a new migratory route. Some of these detours total between 620 and 870 miles, yet they arrive at their intended location.

Red knots teach us that success is more a function of persistence, endurance, planning, and flexibility than size, strength, or natural ability. When success seems too far to reach, the red knot gives us hope.

Love,

Ritchey Marbury

"With ordinary talent and extraordinary perseverance, all things are attainable."

—THOMAS FOWELL BUXTON

REJECT DEBT

Dear Missionaries,

Some have asked if money management is an important part of the gospel. Certainly, how much money you have or do not have will not affect your salvation, but how you use what you have does, and the lessons you teach by your example of money management does. This letter will focus on the importance of money management and suggest ways to do it better.

Some professional counselors say that 80 percent of all families have serious money problems. Others estimate that 89 percent of all divorces begin with quarrels and accusations over money. Elder Marvin J. Ashton, of the Quorum of the Twelve Apostles, taught twelve principles of money management in his April 1975 general conference address. These principles serve both individuals and families. Here they are for your consideration.

1. Pay an honest tithing. Successful financial management begins with payment to the Lord what we owe Him. When we receive our paycheck, and tithing is our first payment, we strengthen our commitment to this principle and reduce our likelihood of mismanagement.
2. Learn to manage money before it manages you. Learning to live within your means is more important than how much money you earn. You gain financial independence

and peace of mind not by how much you make, but by controlling how much you spend.
3. Learn self-discipline and self-restraint in money matters. This can be more important than courses in accounting. Advertisements entice by demonstrating how easy it is to get credit. They fail to focus on paying the money back, how long and hard it will be, and the unavoidable interest added to the original cost.
4. Use a budget. Have a predetermined understanding of how much money is available each month. Know the amount you need to spend on each category of your budget. Carefully record each check when written and balance the checkbook with each monthly bank statement. With the exception of buying a home, paying for an education, and other vital investments, avoid debt and the resulting finance charges. Save and invest a specific percentage of your income.
5. Teach family members early the importance of working and earning. "In the sweat of thy face shalt thou eat bread" (Genesis 3:19) is not outdated counsel. You do a great favor to your children as you teach them to work. Elder Ashton stated that he thinks it is unfortunate for a child to grow up in a home where the seed is planted in the child's mind that there is a family money tree that automatically produces cash once a week or once a month.
6. Teach children to make money decisions in keeping with their capacities to comprehend. Give children the appropriate teaching and individual experience. Then make them responsible for the financial decisions affecting their own money and suffer the consequences of unwise spending. Family unity comes from saving together for a common jointly approved purpose. Rather than teach to save your money, teach to save your money for a mission, bicycle, car, or some specific worthwhile purpose.
7. Teach each family member to contribute to the total family welfare. Let all family members understand the family financial position, budget, and investment goals.

Let them all understand their individual responsibility within the family. Encourage inexpensive fun projects, understandable to the children, that contribute to a family goal or joy.
8. Make education a continuing process. Complete as much formal, full-time education as possible. This includes trade schools and apprentice programs. Such investment brings lifetime potential earnings. Attend night school and correspondence classes. Acquire some special skill you could use to avoid prolonged unemployment. Learn to do basic home and car repairs.
9. Work toward home ownership. Home ownership is an investment. Purchase the type of home your income will support. Improve the home and beautify it throughout the period you occupy the premises.
10. Appropriately involve yourself in an insurance program. Have sufficient medical, automobile, and homeowner's insurance. Have an adequate life insurance program. Costs from illness, accident, and death can financially burden an uninsured family for many years.
11. Understand the influence of external forces on family finances and investments. Inflation offsets a major portion of average wage increases. Larger paychecks may not mean more purchasing power and therefore should not be an excuse for extravagant purchases or additional debt. Avoid all proposals for high-risk investments and get-rich-quick schemes.
12. Appropriately involve yourself in a food storage and emergency preparedness program. Accumulate basic food storage and emergency supplies in a systematic and orderly way, and avoid going in debt for these purposes. Eat nutritious foods and exercise appropriately to improve health, thus avoiding many medical costs.

Elder Ashton warns that these twelve principles are not all inclusive or exclusive. They bring many needs to the surface for consideration. As you free yourself from the bondage of debt, you are better able to set the example for others to see your testimony of the gospel and your determination to live what you learn.

Love,

Ritchey Marbury

"He is rich who owes nothing."

—Hungarian Proverb

Repent And Find Inner Peace

Dear Missionaries,

Repentance is the way provided to be free from sin. Freedom from sin leads to inner peace. We all have a conscience that tells us to refrain from evil. When we are good, we feel good. When we are bad, we feel bad. Inner peace comes from doing what is right consistently, and repenting when we make mistakes.

One little boy in a church primary class listened closely as his teacher taught about repentance. She stressed how good one feels when he or she repents. She talked about how the atonement of Christ takes effect in one's life as he or she repents. She taught how Christ expects us all to repent daily. The young man went home and immediately told his parents he needed to quickly do something bad.

"Why?" questioned the parent.

"So I can repent," replied the child. "I can't think of anything I did wrong today, and my teacher said I must repent daily. I need to do something wrong so I can repent."

We all make mistakes, and that is why we need to repent daily. We may need to correct serious mistakes, or simply recognize we can be better than we are. For the serious mistakes, we need to recognize we did wrong, feel sorrow for our mistakes, and make restitution when possible. We should confess our sins to Heavenly

Father and forsake them. We may need to confess some sins to those leaders called to help us get back on the right path.

We do not need to go about our lives feeling remorse for every little mistake, but it is important to improve every day. Christ told us to be perfect and yet understood that was not possible in this life. We grow toward perfection as we repent. We pray to Heavenly Father and commit to being better tomorrow than we were today. As we repent of our sins, the atonement of Christ becomes effective in our lives—and brings us inner peace.

Love,

Ritchey Marbury

"When I do good, I feel good. When I do bad, I feel bad. That's my religion."

—ABRAHAM LINCOLN

SEARCH THE SCRIPTURES

Dear Missionaries,

Search the scriptures. They testify of Christ. They provide the knowledge necessary for eternal life. They teach the commandments of our Heavenly Father (Heavenly Father's guidelines for happiness). As we keep the commandments, we prosper. As we break them, we fail.

To learn, we read. The scriptures teach us the Plan of Salvation, which Elder Boyd K. Packer called the Lord's Plan of Happiness. They teach us the best way to live. They teach us to understand right from wrong. They teach us the history of those who kept the commandments and those who did not. They teach us mistakes made by many who lived before us.

To understand, we ponder. We think about what we read. We reflect on the lessons taught and how understanding these lessons can benefit our lives. We consider quietly, soberly, and deeply those things we read.

To gain a testimony, we pray. We pray to Heavenly Father in the name of Christ to know the truthfulness of the things we read. We pray with a sincere heart, with real intent, and with faith in Christ. When we do so, we gain a testimony of the truth of these things by the power of the Holy Ghost.

To gain the blessings, we act. The scriptures teach us, "There is a law, irrevocably decreed in heaven before the foundations of this world, upon which all blessings are predicated—And when we obtain any blessing from God, it is by obedience to that law upon which it is predicated" (Doctrine and Covenants 130: 20–21). They also teach us, "I, the Lord, am bound when ye do what I say; but when ye do not what I say, ye have no promise" (Doctrine and Covenants 82:10).

    The scriptures bless us all. We receive those blessings as we read, ponder, pray, and act. That is what it means to "feast upon the words of Christ."

Love,

Ritchey Marbury

"Feast upon the words of Christ; for behold, the words of Christ will tell you all things what ye should do."

—2 NEPHI 32:3

SEE THE GOOD IN CORDELE

Dear Missionaries,

Sunday, August 11, 2013, the *Cordele Dispatch* published this article in their local newspaper. It tells of service by the people of Cordele, Georgia. I wrote the article to show appreciation for the good example set by the many Cordele residents.

SEE THE GOOD IN CORDELE

OK, I'll admit it. I look for the good wherever I go. I am not so naïve as to believe all is rosy; I just prefer looking for the good rather than the ugly, and I find a lot of good in Cordele. Many are embarrassed if their names are mentioned regarding some good deed performed, so I will refrain from doing so in many of these examples; however, good deeds are plentiful in Cordele.

A few weeks ago I attended the Cordele Rotary Club and watched one individual win a drawing worth several hundred dollars. What did he do with his winnings? He donated them back to the club for future service projects.

I talked with a City employee Tuesday morning regarding help needed by one of his neighbors. He told me he gave his neighbor some food and clothing, but wished he could have done more. He just didn't have anything else to give.

He didn't even own a car and he had to walk to work, but he gave his neighbor what he had.

A baseball and basketball official was driving down a street in Highland Grange Subdivision when he spotted a jogger on the side of the road. The official recognized the jogger. He had officiated games when the jogger played basketball in eighth grade and recent games when the jogger, now in the tenth grade, played baseball. The official pulled over to the side of the road, called out to the jogger, and expressed admiration for the young man's continued growth and improvement. The jogger thanked him, smiled, and continued on his way—probably surprised, but pleased, that he was recognized by someone who only knew him from a few sporting events.

This is the kind of people who live and work in Cordele—generous, kind, and thoughtful. It has been that way for years. More than 40 years ago Tony and Martha Jane LaPorte donated a plot of land for what my daughter used to call "Lost in Space," the landmark Titan missile near the intersection of Sixteenth Avenue and I-75. The donation of that land by members of the LaPorte family, and donated efforts by individuals such as John Pate, Billy Raines, and Gene Kelley to erect the missile on the spot where it now stands, continue to remind us all of the good we see in the people of Cordele.

I encourage everyone in this great City of Cordele to look around them for the good. It is easy to see what is wrong, but too often we are so focused on those few isolated incidences that we fail to see the good that occurs here every day. Whether we look for the good or the bad, we will find it; but I am much happier finding the good. How about you?

Love,

Ritchey Marbury

"Whether we look for the good or the bad, we will find it; but I am much happier finding the good. How about you?"

—R<small>ITCHEY</small> M<small>ARBURY</small>

Seek First The Kingdom Of God

Dear Missionaries,

Probably the greatest sermon ever preached was the Sermon on the Mount by the Savior Himself. In Matthew 6:33, He taught to "seek ye first the kingdom of God." Seek requires effort.

In school most wish for perfect scores on every test, but without study, that probably does not happen. Most hope to be successful in work, to advance in salary and authority. If you make no effort, often arrive late, miss work frequently, and do you job sloppily, you will be lucky if you even keep your job.

If you go to the doctor for treatment and the doctor prescribes medication that will cure you, and you fail to follow that advice, your chances for recovery diminish. I went for my annual physical on my birthday a few weeks ago. The doctor told me to lose ten pounds. What did I do? It was my birthday. I went home and had a feast. I then looked at the scales the next morning to find I had gained a few pounds. I wanted to lose the weight but didn't really seek to do so.

If we seek first the Kingdom of God, we must actively seek it rather than just wish for it. As I have probably quoted in other letters, "Work will win when willy wally wishing won't." I don't know who said that, but it is so true.

You find the Sermon on the Mount in Matthew chapters five through seven. Those chapters explain the effort required to seek and find the kingdom of God. Study, ponder, and follow the advice in those chapters, and you will get what you seek.

Love,

Ritchey Marbury

"But seek ye first the kingdom of God, and his righteousness; and all these things shall be added unto you."

—Matthew 6:33

SERMONS WE SEE

Dear Missionaries,

Edgar A. Guest is one of my favorite authors. He teaches wisdom by his poetry. This poem "Sermons We See" is from his book, *The Light of Faith,* published by The Reilly & Lee Company in 1926.

> I'd rather see a sermon
> than hear one any day;
> I'd rather one should walk with me
> than merely tell the way.
> The eye's a better pupil
> and more willing than the ear,
> Fine counsel is confusing,
> but example's always clear;
> And the best of all preachers
> are the men who live their creeds,
> For to see good put in action
> is what everybody needs.
>
> I soon can learn to do it
> if you'll let me see it done;
> I can watch your hands in action,
> but your tongue too fast may run.

Sermons We See

And the lecture you deliver
may be very wise and true,
But I'd rather get my lessons
by observing what you do;
For I might misunderstand you
and the high advice you give,
But there's no misunderstanding
how you act and how you live.

Love,

Ritchey Marbury

"I'd rather see a sermon than hear one any day."

—Edgar A. Guest

Six Days Shalt Thou Work

Dear Missionaries,

Most of us are familiar with the fourth commandment. It tells us to remember the Sabbath day, to keep it holy (Exodus 20:8). We tend to overlook the next verse, however. It reads, "Six days shalt thou labor, and do all thy work" (Exodus 20:9).

When we learn the Ten Commandments, or see them posted on walls or bulletin boards, this ninth verse of Exodus 20 is seldom included, but it is clearly there. We hear a lot of preaching about resting on the Sabbath, and that is good, but what about working the other six weekdays?

Work is a basic principle of the gospel, and is a must for missionary success. We are fortunate when we have the opportunity and health to do something that provides for the needs of life and enriches the circumstances of those around us.

Work is what we make it. If we define work as dull and irksome labor, we make work drudgery. If we define work as labor that is exhausting to the mind and body, we make work a grind. If, however, we define work as sustained mental and physical effort to achieve a worthwhile objective, it is a pursuit. The pursuit of a worthwhile objective is refreshing to both mind and body.

Consider the worker ant. As soon as worker ants are mature and able, they begin working. They first begin caring for the queen and enlarging the nest. Their work is never ending. They forage for food. They bring food back to the nest to feed the colony. When necessary, they fight to defend the colony, and they act as nurses to the young.

As soon as the eggs laid by the ant queen hatch into larvae, the workers immediately act as nurses. They not only feed the oncoming generation, but also watch to maintain proper temperature in their environment. When temperature drops in the evening, they carry the young up near warm stones or pavement. If the day's heat is excessive, they carry the young deeper into the ground. Worker ants are the life blood of the colony, and the colony survives only as the workers do their duty.

Society continues to survive only as long as society continues to work. When young, others nurture and care for us. We would not survive as infants without the careful watchfulness of those who tend to us, feed us, and protect us. As we mature, and are able to take care of ourselves, we have the opportunity to work. Like the worker ant, we have the responsibility to do something that provides for the needs of life and that enriches the circumstances of those around us.

One of the great joys in life is the ability to help those less fortunate than ourselves. Like the worker ant, we often have the opportunity to take care of those who can't take care of themselves. We often have the opportunity to testify of the truthfulness of the true gospel of Jesus Christ.

We appreciate help in our time of need, and at those times wish we could be on the giving side rather than the receiving side. It is in our time of need that, perhaps, we best understand the advice, "It is more blessed to give than to receive."

Work is what we give for the opportunity of living. Like the worker ant, our main purpose in life is to render service. That is also where we find the greatest joy.

Love,

Ritchey Marbury

"The way to be nothing is to do nothing."

—Nathaniel Howe

Smart What?

Dear Missionaries,

This seems to be the age of "smart." We have smart phones. We have smart cars, smart homes, and smart watches. We have smart chairs, smart mattresses, and smart television. In the past we had smart teachers, smart children, and smart parents. The human side of smart seems to be overtaken today by smart computers and other mechanical devices. Yesterday, I even had a salesman try to sell me a smart sanitary sewer manhole cover. In fact the brand name of this device is Smartcover. The crazy thing is that I probably will recommend that various utility departments purchase it.

With all the mechanical smart devices available, are we forgetting the importance of wisdom? Smart implies being mentally alert. Wisdom means having good judgment. Smart means the ability to remember. Wisdom means the ability to apply what we remember in beneficial ways. Smart means knowledge. Wisdom means understanding.

Proverbs 4:7 reads, "Wisdom is the principal thing; therefore get wisdom: and with all thy getting get understanding." Proverbs 9:10 reads, "The fear of the Lord is the beginning of wisdom." With all our smart devices, remember, they are only tools. How we use them determines their real value.

Smart What?

May we never confuse "smart" with "wisdom." James Crichton was one of the smartest men who ever lived. He had a college degree at age thirteen and a master's degree at age fifteen. At age nineteen he challenged all the learned men of Europe to ask questions on any subject in any of ten languages. Using the same language used by the person asking the question, he answered each question fluently. He seemed never to forget anything.

James Crichton was smart but lacked wisdom. With his gift for language, he never wrote a book, a poem, or a song. Though he probably possessed the world's greatest memory, it seems he left nothing for the good of the human race. There is no known record that he accomplished anything. Richly gifted with talent, he died while drunk shortly before age twenty-two. He had the potential for greatness but wasted his talent.

Wisdom comes from God. Greatness comes from following the teachings of Jesus Christ. Smart devices will never replace understanding, and memory will never replace wisdom. Smart devices are tools to use in wise or foolish ways. The choice is ours.

Love,

Ritchey Marbury

"Smart devices will never replace understanding, and memory will never replace wisdom. Smart devices are tools to use in wise or foolish ways. The choice is ours."

—Ritchey Marbury

Spiritually Correct

Dear Missionaries,

I hear a lot these days about being "politically correct." Sometimes the idea is good when it causes us to be more considerate of the way we treat others. Often, however, it seems ridiculous when we feel we have to use terms like "vertically challenged" to mean short, "vertically gifted" to mean tall, "domestic engineer" to mean housewife, or "dining facility" to mean cafeteria.

Some people dislike the word secretary, preferring administrative assistant instead. The word secretary comes from the Medieval Latin word, *secretarius*, meaning "confidential officer." One would think being an "officer" would have more significance than being an "assistant," but nevertheless, many now prefer to be called administrative assistant than secretary.

Swamps are now wetlands, and jungles are rainforests. Illegal aliens are undocumented immigrants, and a broken home is a dysfunctional family. A husband or wife is now a significant other, and bald is follicly challenged.

While we spend much time being politically correct, perhaps we should spend more time being spiritually correct. Political correctness could be defined as using force to change the way we talk in order to attempt to change the way we think. Spiritual correctness could be defined as using free agency to change the way we think in order to help to change the way we talk—and act.

Often the good we would do, we don't, because we don't think about it. As we become spiritually correct, we think of more ways to do good because that is what we want to do. Spiritually correct means being "doers of the word and not hearers only" (James 1:22), but we still need to hear the word and understand the word in order to be doers of the word. As we become spiritually correct, we listen with our ears, study with our minds, and act with our hearts.

Being spiritually correct means changing "my will" to "thy will." It means changing "why me" to "why not me," "shall we help" to "we shall help," and "why pray" to "let's pray."

Political correctness may bring temporal salvation, but spiritual correctness brings eternal salvation. When all is said and done, the correct way is the Savior's way.

Love,

Ritchey Marbury

"Often the good we would do, we don't, because we don't think about it. As we become spiritually correct, we think of more ways to do good because that is what we want to do. As we become spiritually correct, we listen with our ears, study with our minds, and act with our hearts."

—R<small>ITCHEY</small> M<small>ARBURY</small>

Sweet Kiss Of Death

Dear Missionaries,

June 4, 1923, Jockey Frank Hayes raced the horse Sweet Kiss at Belmont Park in New York State. Hayes was thirty-five and had never won a race. His horse was a twenty-to-one outsider owned by Miss A. M. Frayling. That day, however, he won and set a record that probably will never be broken. You see, at the time the horse crossed the finished line, Frank Hayes was dead. Frank Hayes was then, and probably always will be, the only jockey to win a race after death.

Hayes apparently died of a heart attack near the middle of the race. His body somehow stayed in the saddle. The horse crossed the finish line, winning by a head. The horse never raced again, and some claim the horse, Sweet Kiss, was nicknamed "Sweet Kiss of Death" for the rest of its life.

Those nicknaming the horse "Sweet Kiss of Death" told a truth they did not recognize at the time. Death often is sweet. We read in 1 Corinthians 15:55, "O death, where is thy sting? O grave, where is thy victory?" Death is simply a temporary separation of the body from the spirit. After this life we go to a place of everlasting happiness if we live worthy.

We all miss loved ones who depart this temporary mortal existence, but life is forever. This life is a place to gain a body, a place to gain experience, and a place to prepare for an everlasting life. We win the race of life not by how long we live but by how much we give.

Frank Hayes gave his all and won the race even after his death. Jesus Christ gave His all by living a perfect life. In so doing, he atoned for all our weaknesses and mistakes. He made eternal life possible for all as we keep His commandments, which are His guidelines for happiness. There are primarily two commandments: love our Heavenly Father and love one another.

As we finish our mission on this earth, death is like a kiss from our mother. It is sweet because it lets us know we are loved. It brings us from a temporary existence of sweat and toil to a permanent existence of love and happiness.

I love this life, and most of my days are happy ones. My greatest happiness comes from being with my loved ones and friends. My greatest sadness comes when I no longer get to be with those I love so much. Although I am in no hurry to leave this life, I know death will be like a sweet kiss, because death will allow me to be with my friends and loved ones forever.

Love,

Ritchey Marbury

"The briefer life, the earlier immortality."

—Henry Hart Milman

Ten Commandments Today

Dear Missionaries,

Moses, after conversing with the Lord, gave us the Ten Commandments. Exodus 20 relates them. Sometimes we hear them so much we forget they also apply to our day as well as the days of thousands of years ago. Here are some ideas on how they apply to our day.

1. Thou shalt have no other Gods before me. Put Heavenly Father and Jesus Christ before all else—before money, pleasure, and power.
2. Thou shalt not make unto thee any graven image. Worship only our Heavenly Father. Pray to Heavenly Father and no one else.
3. Thou shalt not take the name of the Lord thy God in vain. This is self-explanatory, but it also reminds us to "swear not at all" (Matthew 5:34) as Jesus taught in the Sermon on the Mount.
4. Remember the Sabbath day, to keep it holy. The Sabbath is the Lord's Day. We honor it on the first day of the week because Christ rose from the dead on the first day of the week. This is a day to rest from our worldly pursuits and focus on those things that bring us closer to Christ and our Heavenly Father.

5. Honor thy father and thy mother. Remember, if it were not for them, we would not be born on this earth. They gave us life. They are due our love, respect, and consideration.
6. Thou shalt not kill. Murder of innocent people is one of the most grievous of sins. Christ added the warning in Matthew 5:22 that whosoever is angry with others without cause is in danger of judgment, and whoever shall say, "Thou fool," shall be in danger of hellfire.
7. Thou shalt not commit adultery. Christ also taught in Matthew 5:28 that "whosoever looketh on a woman to lust after her hath committed adultery with her already in his heart."
8. Thou shalt not steal. Those who steal possessions are in danger of punishment by civil laws. Those who steal another's good name may not get the same punishment in this life, but doing so may be even more serious in the Lord's eyes. Do not steal others' possessions, their good name, their chastity, or any other thing belonging to them.
9. Thou shalt not bear false witness. Jesus added in Matthew 7:1–2 that we should be careful not to judge, for we shall be judged with those same judgments we judge. In other words, be truthful in all dealings.
10. Thou shalt not covet. Be grateful for your own blessings. Do not desire or strive to obtain that which belongs to another.

Commandments from the Lord are guidelines for happiness. Happiness comes when we obey, and sadness comes when we disobey. I want to be happy. Don't you?

Love,

Ritchey Marbury

"Those who are not governed by God will be ruled by Tyrants."

—William Penn

Thanks For Gnats

Dear Missionaries,

I am thankful for the little things in life—kisses from my wife, hugs from my children and grandchildren, encouragement from parents and friends, a simple thank you, and a smile. When I am annoyed by little gnats in summertime, I remember how we are most influenced by the little things in life.

I am thankful for my wife, and prior to our marriage, I would sometimes give her orchids. Gnats, I discovered, help pollinate some South American orchids that allow them to produce the flowers I gave my sweetheart on special occasions.

I am thankful for summertime. Winter is fine, but we need warm weather to enjoy sports like swimming and water skiing. Gnats only come out in warm weather, so when we see gnats, we know it is time to play.

I am thankful that where I live there is an abundance of water. I read of people dying in deserts because they have no water to drink. Where there are gnats there is water, because gnat larvae live in moist environments.

I am thankful for special events and festivals where I can have a good time with my friends and family. One of the best festivals in the South is "Gnat Days." The first weekend in May the City of Camilla, Georgia, celebrates these tiny insects with a fabulous festival. It features Gnat Day bike races, a taster's luncheon, a gnat market, a merchant's sale, and a Saturday night "Under the Oakes" dance.

I am thankful for the opportunity of good conversation. Down South, if you can't think of anything else to talk about, you can talk about gnats. To those who live above the "gnat line," you can explain how to extend your lower lip beyond your upper lip and send a blast of air upward to blow away the pesky insects.

I am thankful for good health. Gnats are generally a detriment to good health, and so I am thankful when they are no longer around. Sometimes it takes discomfort to appreciate the good times.

I am thankful for so many things: the burdens that I didn't have to bear, the joys that didn't perish, the bitter words unspoken, the laughter from both little children and senior citizens, and the love of our Heavenly Father and Jesus Christ. And yes, I am even thankful for gnats.

> Love,
>
> Ritchey Marbury

> *"And let the peace of God rule in your hearts, to the which also ye are called in one body; and be ye thankful."*
>
> —COLOSSIANS 3:15

Things Jesus Taught

Dear Missionaries,

Jesus taught us many things, not only in words, but by example. During His last week as a mortal, He taught His disciples, "This is my commandment, that ye love one another, as I have loved you" (John 15:12). He taught, "Greater love hath no man than this, that a man lay down his life for his friends" (John 15:13). He then gave His life for each of us.

Jesus taught by example how to be kind and loving. He went about doing good. He healed the sick, made the blind to see, and the lame to walk. When His disciples rebuked those who brought little children to Him, he responded by saying, "Suffer the little children to come unto me, and forbid them not; for of such is the kingdom of God" (Mark 10:14). Jesus taught to "love your enemies, bless them that curse you, do good to them that hate you, and pray for them which despitefully use you and persecute you" (Matthew 5:44).

Jesus taught obedience to His Father in Heaven. Even though He was sinless, He traveled to Jordan to be baptized by John. When John forbade Him, Jesus responded, "Suffer it to be so now; for thus it becometh us to fulfil all righteousness" (Matthew 3:15). In the Garden of Gethsemane, Jesus prayed, "Father, if thou be willing, remove this cup from me; nevertheless not my will, but thine, be done" (Luke 22:42).

Jesus taught the importance of scripture study. When led into the wilderness to be tempted by the devil, He responded to each temptation by quoting scripture. When the tempter told Him to turn stone into bread, Jesus answered, "It is written, man shall not live by bread alone, but by every word that proceedeth out of the mouth of God" (Matthew 3:4). When tempted to cast Himself down from the pinnacle of the temple, Jesus answered, "It is written, Thou shalt not tempt the Lord thy God" (Matthew 4:7). When Satan attempted to get Jesus to worship him, Jesus answered, "Get thee hence, Satan: for it is written, thou shalt worship the Lord thy God, and Him only shalt thou serve" (Matthew 4:10).

Jesus taught how to forgive. When the scribes and Pharisees brought Jesus a woman taken in adultery and demanded she be stoned to death as prescribed by the law of Moses, Jesus first told the crowd to let those without sin cast the first stone. After her accusers went away, Jesus told the woman that He, also, would not condemn her. She should go and sin no more.

Even when dying on the cross, Jesus looked down on the soldiers taking part in His crucifixion and prayed, "Father, forgive them; for they know not what they do" (Luke 23:34).

Jesus taught us many more things by His example and words. Perhaps if we can remember and do just a few of these things, our lives will grow richer.

Love,

Ritchey Marbury

"For God sent not His Son into the world to condemn the world; but that the world through Him might be saved."

—JOHN 3:17

Thoughts On Life

Dear Missionaries,

Ray Jensen, Bob Oates, and I served in the Georgia District presidency from late 1970 until the middle of 1972. Ray Jensen, the district president, wrote a monthly message on the front page of a four-page newsletter, which we mailed to all members in our district. On January 1971, President Jensen wrote a message entitled "Some Thoughts on Life." The message is powerful and is included here.

SOME THOUGHTS ON LIFE

The greatest sin—Fear
The best day—Today
The best town—Where you succeed
The most agreeable companion—One who would not have you other than you are
The greatest bore—One who keeps on talking after making his point
The greatest deceiver—the one who deceives himself
The greatest invention of the devil—War
The greatest comfort—a job well done
The greatest mistake—Giving up
The most intensive indulgence—Hate

The greatest trouble maker—He who talks too much
The greatest stumbling block—Egotism
The most ridiculous trait—Being self-impressed
The most dangerous person—the liar
The greatest need—Common sense
The greatest puzzle—Life
The greatest mystery—Death
The greatest thought—God
The greatest thing of all, bar none, in this world—Love

President Jensen then asked in his letter to consider some words of Goethe, one of the greatest poet-philosophers of our time, on nine wishes for a successful life.

"Health enough to make work a pleasure
Wealth enough to support your needs
Strength enough to battle with difficulties and overcome them
Grace enough to confess your sins and forsake them
Patience enough to toil until some good is accomplished
Charity enough to see some good in your neighbor
Love enough to move you to be useful and helpful to others
Faith enough to make real the things of God
Hope enough to remove all anxious fears concerning the future."

He ended his monthly message with these words from theologian Dr. Reinhold Niebuhr: "Grant me the serenity to accept the things I cannot change; the courage to change the things I can; and the wisdom to know the difference."

Ray Jensen was born September 28, 1917, and died April 17, 2013, at age ninety-five. He taught me many things. I miss him.

Love,

Ritchey Marbury

"Tragedy is something of an intellectual matter until we experience it."

—E. Ray Jensen

To Thine Own Self Be True

Dear Missionaries,

In his immortal work, *Hamlet*, William Shakespeare had Polonius give advice to his son, Laertes. Though he wrote these words more than four hundred years ago, the advice is good today. In today's English he tells his son to keep thoughts to oneself, be friendly but not vulgar, have friends but do not take advantage of them, avoid confrontation when possible, listen more and talk less, listen to ideas from others but reserve judgment, dress appropriately, do not borrow nor lend, and be true to yourself.

Here are these thoughts in Shakespeare's own words:

> Give thy thoughts no tongue,
> Nor any unproportion'd thought his act.
> Be thou familiar, but by no means vulgar.
> Those friends thou hast, and their adoption tried,
> Grapple them to thy soul with hoops of steel;
> But do not dull thy palm with entertainment
> Of each new-hatch'd, unfledged comrade. Beware
> Of entrance to a quarrel; but being in,
> Bear't that the opposed may beware of thee.
> Give every man thy ear, but few thy voice;
> Take each man's censure, but reserve thy judgment.
> Costly thy habit as thy purse can buy,

But not express'd in fancy; rich, not gaudy;
For the apparel oft proclaims the man,
And they in France of the best rank and station
Are of a most select and generous, chief in that.
Neither a borrower nor a lender be;
For loan oft loses both itself and friend,
And borrowing dulls the edge of husbandry.
This above all: to thine own self be true,
And it must follow, as the night the day,
Thou canst not then be false to any man.

Joseph Smith taught to "seek ye out of the best books words of wisdom; seek learning, even by study and also by faith" (Doctrine and Covenants 88:118). Our first priority for study should always be the scriptures—the words of Christ and Heavenly Father as given to apostles and prophets. As we study other of the best books, the works of Shakespeare are worth considering.

Love,

Ritchey Marbury

"This above all: to thine own self be true,
And it must follow, as the night the day,
Thou canst not then be false to any man."

—WILLIAM SHAKESPEARE

TOGETHER IN LIFE AND ETERNITY

Dear Missionaries,

About 9:30 a.m. Saturday, August 29, 2015, Arva Joy Ward Williams simply stopped breathing and returned to her Heavenly Father, to her Savior, Jesus Christ, and to her husband, William Hillman Williams. Hillman, her husband, departed this life May 6, 2015, a little less than four months earlier. They lived together, on this earth, as husband and wife for sixty-four years. They now have an eternity to enjoy life together.

Jesus told His apostles in John 14: 1–3, "Let not your heart be troubled: ye believe in God, believe also in me. In my Father's house are many mansions: if it were not so, I would have told you. I go to prepare a place for you. And if I go to prepare a place for you, I will come again, and receive you unto myself; that where I am, there ye may be also."

Although Jesus spoke these words to His apostles, Hillman could well have spoken these words to Arva. They were sealed for time and all eternity in the Holy Temple and knew that the sacred bonds of matrimony continue from this life through the next. That is one of the great blessings of understanding the true gospel of Jesus Christ as taught by the Church of Jesus Christ of Latter-day Saints.

Theodore M. Burton, in a past general conference address, spoke of a question his cousin Rodney Moyle asked him. He asked if Elder Burton had his heart's desire and could take it with him out of this world, what would it be?

Elder Burton replied, "My family and loved ones."

The gospel of Jesus Christ promises just that to those who are faithful to Christ's teachings. It answers the questions, "Where did I come from? Why am I here? Where am I going after this life is over?"

Acts 17:29 tells us, "We are the offspring of God." That is where we came from. We come from a loving Heavenly Father.

We are here to gain a body, to gain experience, and to nourish others. We are here to provide nourishment for the body and love for the soul. That is why we are here.

After this life is over, we go to a better existence, a continuation of life. The definition of death is not the end, but a temporary separation—a temporary separation of the body and the spirit. Just as we miss our loved ones when they leave us temporarily for a long vacation, we also rejoice knowing we will see them again. We grieve when our loved ones leave this life for the next, but we rejoice knowing we will see them again as we are faithful.

Knowledge of everlasting and eternal life comes through prayer, through communion with our Heavenly Father. Christ told us he would come again to receive us unto Himself. When Mary and others approached the tomb of Jesus, two men in shining garments spoke to them, saying, "Why seek ye the living among the dead? He is not here, but is risen" (Luke 24:5–6).

Paul in 1 Corinthians 15:5–8 tells us many saw the resurrected Christ, including Cephas, about five hundred brethren, James, and all of the apostles. The Book of Mormon tells us how about 2,500 saw the resurrected Christ. Joseph Smith saw Christ and witnessed to that fact in Doctrine and Covenants 76:22–23. Christ does live, and because of His life and atonement for us, we all shall inherit everlasting life.

Arva once told her son, Dave, as he drove her along a small road and veered off due to inattention, "You need to get on the road." The road to eternal life with our family and loved ones is the one that follows Christ's teachings. Arva had it right.

Love,

Ritchey Marbury

"You need to get on the road."

—A<small>RVA</small> W<small>ILLIAMS</small>

Tribute to Mother

Dear Missionaries,

John Greenleaf Whittier wrote this little poem, "Tribute to Mother," many years ago. At Mother's Day and every day, this poem seems fitting.

> A picture memory brings to me;
> I look across the years and see
> Myself beside my mother's knee.
>
> I feel her gentle hand restrain
> My selfish moods, and know again
> A child's blind sense of wrong and pain.
>
> But wiser now, a man gray grown,
> My childhood's needs are better known.
> My mother's chastening love I own.

Love,

Ritchey Marbury

"Most of all the other beautiful things in life come by twos and threes, by dozens and hundreds. Plenty of roses, stars, sunsets, rainbows, brothers and sisters, aunts and cousins, but only one mother in the whole world."

—Kate Douglas Wiggin

Ugly Purple Scarf

Dear Missionaries,

Of all the Christmas presents I have given my wife, Fonda, in our more than fifty years of marriage, perhaps an ugly purple scarf is the most memorable. I gave it to her Christmas, 1978, and now, almost forty years later, she still uses it.

It was our first Christmas in Idaho serving as mission president and companion in the Idaho Pocatello Mission. (The mission headquarters would move to Boise the following year and become the Idaho Boise Mission.) We had little money, and all I could afford to spend was five dollars. I purchased a nail file, a comb, and a purple scarf. That was her total Christmas present. I thought the scarf was pretty. Fonda called it ugly. She still calls it her "ugly purple scarf."

I don't know what became of the nail file and comb, but she still uses the "ugly purple scarf." She places it over her hair to avoid getting makeup on her blouse as she pulls her blouse over her head. Neither of us remember what I received for Christmas that year, nor do we remember what either of us received on many Christmases after that. We both remember the scarf. I used what little money I had to get her the best gift I could afford. What made the gift special was the love that went with the gift.

The real value of any gift is the love it represents. William Sidney Porter, more commonly known as O. Henry, in his short story "The

Gift of the Magi" tells of Jim and Della. They had few possessions, but they did have two in which they took mighty pride. One was Jim's gold watch, and the other was Della's hair. For Christmas one year, Jim sold his gold watch to buy Della tortoise combs for her hair. Della cut her hair to buy Jim a platinum fob chain for his watch. Though neither gift served its intended purpose, the real value was the love demonstrated that memorable day.

Christmas is a time when we celebrate the love our Heavenly Father has for us. He gave His only begotten Son that all of us could have everlasting life, that all of us could return and live with Him after this mortal life is over. Jesus Christ agreed to come to this earth and suffer a pain only He could endure, that we might not suffer as He did.

We read in John 3:16–17, "For God so loved the world, that he gave his only begotten Son, that whosoever believeth in him should not perish, but have everlasting life. For God sent not his Son into the world to condemn the world; but that the world through him might be saved."

We observe Christmas with bright lights, decorations, and festivities. We celebrate Christmas with fun, merriment, and banquets; but we keep Christmas with gift giving, remembering the Savior and following His teachings.

Love,

Ritchey Marbury

"The real value of any gift is the love it represents."

—Ritchey Marbury

Venus Flytrap—Nature's Deadly Tantalizer

Dear Missionaries,

 In North Carolina's Green Swamp grows a flower of unusual beauty and charm, especially to small ants and spiders. The plant takes four or five years to reach maturity, but in the right conditions, lives twenty to thirty years. Its structure is a rosette of four to seven leaves arising from a short bulblike stem. Its sweet sap lures unsuspecting ants, spiders, beetles, grasshoppers and a few flying insects to crawl along its leaves and touch one of the tiny hairs located on its inner surface.

 You can find this plant, the Venus flytrap, within a sixty-mile radius of Wilmington, North Carolina. A few are found in northern Florida, western Washington, and other areas of nitrogen- and phosphorus poor environments. Due to the poor soil conditions in which it lives, it looks for other sources of nitrogen. This comes from its diet of living creatures. They include 33 percent ants, 30 percent spiders, 10 percent beetles, 10 percent grasshoppers, and fewer than 5 percent flying insects.

 As an unsuspecting critter touches one of the trigger hairs, the trap is ready. It reacts like a time bomb. The timer is set to twenty seconds. If the victim touches the second hair before the twenty seconds expire—snap—one-tenth of a second later the lobes of the trap shut. Stiff hairlike protrusions called cilia mesh together. Holes in the meshwork allow small prey to escape, but as larger prey struggle to escape, the trap tightens, and digestion quickens.

As the prey continues to move, it stimulates the inner surface of the lobes, forcing the edges of the lobes together. The trap is sealed. Enzymes secreted by glands in the lobes speed up the digestive process. About ten days later, digestion is complete. The prey becomes a small husk; the trap reopens, and the plant waits for its next victim.

Watch out for spiritual flytraps. They are even more deadly. Small indiscretions, a white lie, a few crude words, failure to help a struggling friend—when these become habits, they also become spiritual flytraps. It may take them four or five years to become habits, but the habits can last a lifetime. The habits seem harmless; but habits, good or bad, are hard to break.

Spiritual flytraps lurk wherever conditions are poor for hearing messages from Heavenly Father. They are in R-rated movies, Internet porn sites, and drug-related hangouts. They may come from a diet of drugs, alcohol, or riotous living.

As you unexpectedly partake of these vices, the trap is ready. It reacts like a time bomb. First, you find one unwholesome activity. Then you add another. You are hooked on the habit, and the trap is sealed. The wickedness has its victim. When the habit is small, confessing and forsaking brings relief. Struggling to escape by lying and trying to hide your mistake only tightens the trap.

If you continue to struggle without repenting, Satan will digest you, and you will be lost. But there is a way out. Unlike the struggling prey digested by the Venus flytrap, hope for redemption is never lost. Our Savior, Jesus Christ, provided the way. He taught that if we will repent of our sins, forsake them, and ask our Heavenly Father for forgiveness, he will forgive us. He said He would not only forgive us but He would remember our sins no more. Happiness and peace of mind will return, and once again you will find the joy of knowing you are a child of God. Satan will continue to wait for his next victim, but it will not be you.

Love,

Ritchey Marbury

"The only safe ground is so far from danger as it is possible to get."

—HEBER J. GRANT

Wanting To Or Willing To

Dear Missionaries,

"And he went a little further, and fell on his face, and prayed, saying, O my Father, if it be possible, let this cup pass from me: nevertheless not as I will, but as thou wilt" (Matthew 26:39).

The Lord does not require us to want to do all things He asks. He only requires us to be willing. Christ did not want to suffer the pains and agony He suffered. In fact, He asked His Father to remove that requirement. Nevertheless, He was willing to do all things required by His Father in Heaven, and He did.

K. R. Ravindran, president of Rotary International from July 2015 through June 2016, tells of an experience he had many years ago when he met Mother Teresa. He said he asked her about her greatest achievement. She answered that she was an expert at cleaning toilets. She may not have wanted to clean toilets, but she saw the need and was willing to do it.

One day an airline director had tickets for a flight Mother Teresa requested. When he found her, Mother Teresa, thinking he was a volunteer, handed him a brush, explained how best to clean toilets, and left him standing there, brush in hand. Expensive suit and all, the director went to work cleaning toilets. Later he again approached Mother Teresa with a small envelope.

"Mother Teresa," he said, "I have finished cleaning the toilets. May I speak with you now?"

"Yes, certainly," she said.

"Mother Teresa, I am the director of the airline, and here are your tickets. I just wanted to bring them to you personally."

That airline director did not want to clean toilets but was willing. In so doing, he said those twenty minutes cleaning toilets filled him with one of the greatest joys he had ever known. As we willingly do the right thing, often that experience helps us understand its importance, and we want to do more.

Love,

Ritchey Marbury

"Yesterday is gone. Tomorrow has not yet come. We have only today. Let us begin."

—MOTHER TERESA

What Is The Price?

Dear Missionaries,

A friend of mine purchased a new car recently, telling me that it cost him nothing since the monthly payments would be the same as he was paying on his current car. I asked him the total cost of his new car. He didn't know. He only knew the monthly payments. I asked him how long he would be making those payments. Again, he didn't know.

Another friend acquired a mobile phone at no cost—or so she thought. The phone, indeed, was free, but it came with a yearly contract to use a certain service at a fee considerably higher than monthly payments from similar companies. She could have purchased the same phone from another company with lower monthly service charges. At the end of the year, her total would have been less had she purchased the phone and contracted for the lower monthly service charge.

Each friend received immediate gratification but was lulled into long-term commitments. So it is with many of Satan's ploys. He entices us with immediate pleasure and long-term consequences. There is no credit buying in the Lord's kingdom. In the Lord's kingdom, we pay the price first and receive long-term rewards.

Certainly an eternal life with our loved ones is better than a few moments of carnal pleasure. Self-control during times of stress is better than temper tantrums. Sugar and candy taste great, but too much can be a weighty problem.

When we know the price, we make better decisions. There is a price for every action, and every decision requires the sacrifice of some alternative. We choose the action, and the consequences follow, good or bad. May we always determine the true price before every decision, and thereby make wise choices.

Love,

Ritchey Marbury

"For the wages of sin is death; but the gift of God is eternal life through Jesus Christ our Lord."

—Romans 6:23

What Is The Risk?

Dear Missionaries,

Several years ago there lived a woman so afraid of failure she determined to take no risk in life. She never married, for she was afraid she would get a husband who would beat her, verbally abuse her, or laugh at her. She never had children, for she never married and would never get involved with any man. She never confided in anyone for fear someone would betray her confidence.

Ruth Mason Rice must have known someone like that when she wrote her poem, "Risky Business."

> *It's a risk to have a husband, a risk to have a son;*
> *A risk to pour confidences out to anyone;*
> *A risk to pick a daisy, for there's sure to be a cop;*
> *A risk to go on living, but a greater risk to stop.*

Life is a risk. Every decision is a risk, and every decision requires the sacrifice of some alternative. The question is not whether or not to take risk, but whether or not the risk is worth taking.

A mother takes risks every time she gives birth to a new baby. A firefighter takes risks every time he or she enters a burning building. A doctor takes risks every time he or she treats a patient with a contagious disease.

A motorist takes risks that no accident will occur while driving. Every airplane flight runs the risk of crash. Every boat cruise runs the risk of a sinking ship.

We risk stubbing our toe with every step, but we don't stop walking. We risk inhaling polluted air every time we take a breath, but we don't stop breathing. We risk debris blowing into our eyes every time we walk in the sand, but we don't walk with our eyes closed.

Heavenly Father took the risk that the world would not listen to or follow His son, but He sent Him anyway, that we all would have the opportunity to live with Him forever. Jesus Christ took the risk that His enemies would crucify him. They did. He knew they would, but he loved us so much He willingly gave His life to save ours. We risk the ridicule of foolish people when we choose to follow the Savior in all of His teachings, but the reward of doing so is eternal life.

Life without risk is dull. There is, however, no life without risk, and often the risk we choose determines our quality of life.

Love,

Ritchey Marbury

"It's a risk to go on living, but a greater risk to stop."

—Ruth Mason Rice

WHY ME?

Dear Missionaries,

In the spring of 1980, I spoke to a group of students at the LDS Institute in Boise, Idaho. I did not know they were recording the speech, but they were. Fonda and I were serving then as mission president and companion of the Idaho Boise Mission. I found a copy of this speech the other day and decided to include it here. It was called "Why Me?"

There comes a time in the lives of all people when they must seal, with their actions, their testimony of those principles in which they believe. There comes a time in the lives of all people when they must sacrifice to maintain those blessings they hold most sacred. And there comes a time in the lives of all people when they must cease to ask the question, "Why me?" and start asking the question, "Why not me?" Well, that time is now.

It has been said that luck is when opportunity meets preparation. We've been told how important it is to prepare—to live the words of the Savior and to prepare ourselves spiritually, physically, and mentally. We know that preparation is, to a large degree, perspiration. We know it requires work. We know that it is important for us to live our lives so that when our time of opportunity comes, we will be prepared. My suggestion to you, now, is to prepare yourself. Your time will come.

Why Me?

I thought I might simply speak informally to you and discuss some things that have happened to people. First, missionaries within this mission who were prepared when their time came—more essentially, who were prepared spiritually. Missionaries who had learned to ask the question, "Why not me?"

Each of the things that I'll be talking about are things that did happen right here in this mission. Things that happened to people that I have been personally acquainted with. Experiences that I have been able to see. Experiences that I've recognized and I've been able to certify to because I've been a part of them. Experiences that prove these people were prepared and recognized that when the time of opportunity comes, the time of preparation is over. They were prepared, and their time came.

The first instance—I won't give the names because many of the missionaries are still out in the mission, many of the people involved are still here, and some of the events are rather sacred to them, so they probably would rather not have their names mentioned. Each of these experiences are true and have occurred within the time that I've been on my mission. It was in the last twenty months or so.

Not long after I came out on my mission, we had a missionary arrive. The missionary told me the story of his father and how he came out on his mission. His father had a very rare disease called myasthenia gravis. Many of you have never heard of that disease. It is so rare that many doctors feel that if they treat three or four patients, they have had a great deal of experience. Extremely rare. It's a disease of the muscles that causes you to have absolutely no control over your body movement. The man that had this disease, this young man's father, couldn't raise his arms; he couldn't move his legs. He even had difficulty holding his eyelids open. That's how serious the disease was.

He couldn't move his neck, and he had to wear a neck brace. He couldn't swallow because he didn't even have control of the muscles that allow him to swallow. He couldn't speak, although he could mumble enough to communicate, but very unintelligibly. It was very difficult to understand him.

This man, of course, wasn't able to earn the income necessary to send his son on a mission, but his son wanted to go. The bishop wanted him to be able to go.

After prayer, the bishop came to this man and said, "Brother, we have a calling for you in the Church. Of course, the young man's father looked at him questioningly, and then the answer was, "The calling that we have for you is to be assistant ward clerk."

The young man's father forced as much of a smile as he could, thinking to himself, "Now isn't that silly! Here I am, I can't even move my fingers. I can't even swallow, and they're calling me to be assistant ward clerk. A job that requires me to be able to see, and I can't hold by eyelids open. A job that requires me to have at least enough manual dexterity to be able to write numbers and add them back and forth. There's no way I can do it."

The bishop said again, "Brother So and So, we're calling you to be the assistant ward clerk, and this is a call from the Lord."

The missionary related to me how his father explained that he remembered how his Patriarchial Blessing promised if he would accept any calling that he received, that the Lord would bless him to the extent that he would be able to fulfill that calling. He thought to himself, "Well, I don't know how much faith I really have, but if I accept it, the Lord has to heal me for me to be able to act as an assistant ward clerk. I really can't lose anything. I don't like the idea of being a clerk. If I had my druthers, I think the last calling I'd want in the Church would be that of a clerk."

Then he thought, "I'll do it.I'll put the Lord to the test." He indicated to the bishop as best he could that he would accept the call.

Then the bishop did something. The bishop exercised faith. I wonder how many bishops have this much faith. The bishop said, "I also feel impressed that I should give you a blessing. Will it be all right?"

The man nodded yes. The bishop then put his hands on the head of that father and said, "By the authority of the priesthood which I hold, and in the name of Jesus Christ, I command your body to be made whole."

Now here's a man that's dying. Myasthenia gravis is a disease for which there is no known cure. Here is a bishop talking to a man who has been told by all the competent medical authorities in the area that he was going to die. The bishop commands this man's body to be made whole and promises him health. Then he leaves.

I learned the rest of that story shortly after the son was on his mission. I received a phone call, and it was from the young man's father. I had heard this story, so I told the man, "I'm surprised to hear you are able to speak. Your son told me that you had myasthenia. I had a friend that died of that disease."

I didn't mean to discourage him, but sometimes my choice of words is not what it should be. I asked, "Well, how are you doing? How are you feeling?"

He replied, "I can best answer that by telling you that I'm a barber. (That requires some manual dexterity.) My business is going so well that I've just opened a second business."

"In other words, you are cured?"

"Yes," he said. "It didn't happen all at once. I accepted the call, and suddenly I found that I could make every meeting and I was able to be an assistant ward clerk. I found that all of a sudden I was getting better."

Then he said, "I didn't really realize exactly what had happened and the extent of the blessings. So I quit going to church for a little while. You know, I was back in bed again. I repented of that, and went back to my calling as assistant ward clerk, and I haven't had any problems since."

I said, "I'll bet you haven't missed any meetings since either, have you?" Of course, his answer was, "I sure haven't!" (Note: I saw this man's son again in October, 2016. The son told me his father was still alive and doing well.)

You see what can happen when you are really prepared? When you are spiritually in tune as this bishop was, you can demonstrate the power of God by your actions.

This bishop, when the Lord gave him a message, acted on it. He knew what it meant to pray. He understood how to be receptive to prayer. This bishop, in answer to a commandment from the Lord, walked over to a dying man and commanded his body to be made whole, and it happened. It happened because that bishop said, "Why not me?" rather than "Why me?"

Another example happened about a year ago. Two missionaries were teaching a young lady—probably in her middle twenties. She was expecting a baby, and she had a very serious concern. She had been told by her doctor that she had cancer and there was concern whether or not she would live. Even more serious than that, there was concern on the part of this lady whether or not her yet-to-be-born baby would live.

The lady expressed that her concern wasn't nearly so much for her own life as for the life of her unborn baby. During the process of the discussions, the missionaries taught how the apostles of old were able to give blessings and people were restored to health.

The lady said, "If the apostles of old could do it, and this is the true church and you represent the Savior, why can't you cure me?"

She asked in faith for these two missionaries to give her a blessing. They did. Then they left. The next day, the lady went to the hospital. She was examined again to see how far the cancer had progressed and to set a date for an operation. After the examination, the doctor said, "I don't understand it. Somehow in the last few days, a miracle has occurred. Your cancer has reversed itself. It is now smaller than the head of a pin. We can probably do nothing, and it will simply go away. If you would like, we can operate, but now it is so small that it will be a minor operation. In fact, so minor that we can assure you good health. We can also assure your baby to born in good health."

The example I just gave you occurred in the east end of this mission. Another example—over in the west end of the mission. A missionary, this time going out with a team teacher, was over in an area visiting a man to teach him about the gospel. They asked him to be baptized, and the man said that he wouldn't be able to, that he probably wouldn't live that long.

It was explained to the missionaries that this man, also, had cancer, but it was much more serious. The man had a cancerous growth behind his left ear. It was growing so rapidly, and it was so serious, that the man had already obtained total blindness in his left eye and partial blindness in his right eye. The doctor's expectation was that this man would not live more than two weeks. There was, however, a specialist in Portland, Oregon, who could perhaps perform an operation that would extend his life for a few months so that he could get his affairs in order.

In order to keep the man's hopes from getting too high, they explained very frankly that there was no way that his life could be saved—the cancer had gone too far. He would die, but perhaps they could extend his life a month or two. The man was preparing to leave the next day to go for the emergency operation when the missionaries were there. They taught him, and they also explained the principles of faith. They explained the power of commitment and how the Lord blesses those who are sincere. They asked him if he wanted to be baptized, and he said yes, but he felt he needed to go for the operation first, and he didn't know if he would make it back. He then asked for a blessing.

Now listen to this. Here's a man who is literally dying of a disease just as deadly—in fact, more deadly—than the leprosy that we hear about all through the scriptures.

Here's a man who has cancer so far progressed that he is blind in his left eye and partially blind in his right eye. This missionary and his team teacher laid their hands on the head of this man, and the missionary sealed the blessing, saying, "By the power of the Holy Priesthood which we hold, and in the name of Jesus Christ, we command your body to be made whole." Then they left.

The next morning when the man awoke to get ready for his trip, he knew something was different. Not only was his vision now perfect in his right eye, which had been partially blind, but he also was able to see out of his left eye. His vision had been restored. He didn't understand it, but he knew that there was something that was happening within his body, and he felt better.

He left and was rushed to the specialist in Portland, Oregon. The specialist observed him, then others were probably brought in. After some deliberation, they told the man they wanted to have a conference with him. The doctor said, "We don't understand it. A miracle has occurred. The cancer in your body has died. Not only that, you're well. You're cured. We haven't done anything. We don't know what happened, except we know that you're cured. You go back home and live a good life and just thank the Lord for your blessings."

He went back, and as you can imagine, he was baptized just a few days later.

The point is, here were some missionaries who were working hard, were dedicated, had prepared themselves spiritually, as well as mentally, emotionally, and physically, and were not afraid to demonstrate the power of the Lord. Here were some missionaries who lived so close to their Heavenly Father that they were able to read the scriptures and to exhibit the same faith as the prophets of old who had performed miracles.

They didn't say, "Why me?" They simply said, "Why not me?" They demonstrated the power of the Lord and received the blessings that come from having faith and living a proper life.

Another example. I told this to the missionaries not too long ago. We had two missionaries who were very concerned about the people that they could bring into the gospel. They had taught the gospel to a number of people but were not having any success. The people weren't accepting the messages as they felt they should. So the missionaries said, "All right, we'll prepare ourselves through prayer and fasting."

This incident happened on February 17. They fasted, knelt down, prayed, and asked the Lord to bless them by putting them in contact with someone who was ready to hear the message they were about to present. After fasting for the noon and evening meals, they went to sleep.

At 3:00 a.m., the phone rang. It was a bishop on the other end of the line saying that someone had called the hot line and asked to speak to some ministers, preferably missionaries. By 3:30 a.m., the missionaries were teaching the individual.

They taught him for a while, went back home, and got a couple hours' sleep, then went back. They met with him around eight that morning, and for five hours they continued to teach him the principles of the gospel. Seven days later, February 24, that individual was baptized.

I told about that incident at our last zone conference in Twin Falls. This morning I received a phone call from a missionary over in Twin Falls, and he said, "President Marbury, do you remember telling us about what happened to the missionaries who prayed and fasted?"

I said, "Yes."

He said, "Well, I want to tell you an experience we had. We had eight people committed to be baptized, and when we went over to see them, things had occurred that made them where they wouldn't qualify for baptism right now. Probably a little bit later, but not right now. Their baptism would probably have to be postponed a week. You know, President, we were just so committed to having seven or eight baptisms that we decided to do the same things those missionaries did, and we prayed and asked the Lord if He wouldn't bless us to present our message to some that were really prepared to hear it. Then we went to bed.

"Interestingly enough," they said, "at three this morning, we received a phone call." (I guess we find the spirit works best at three in the morning.) A lady on the phone asked them if they could come over to her house. She said, "We're having some problems, and we would like to talk with you."

He didn't remember the name. He didn't know just exactly who it was but asked the lady how she knew who he was. He had been tracting throughout the area, had gone to their home, and they had refused to let him in. He had continued his work, not really thinking too much about it. Later that night, the problems were occurring in this family, and they felt a need to have counsel from a minister.

They knew some ministers in the area, but they had felt a good spirit from this young missionary who had come by the door, even though they hadn't let him in. They had remembered his name and in some way were able to find his telephone number. In their hour of need, the Lord had somehow directed them to call this missionary. He and his companion went to the home of the family and taught them.

As the elder talked to me at six thirty in the morning, he explained, "And you know what, President? There are seven of them that are committed to be baptized this coming Sunday. They're so strong. It seems that we have been able to save their family relationship. Not only that, they have accepted the gospel, and perhaps we have provided them with some eternal blessings."

Now here are the things that can happen when you are prepared, when you really love the Lord. Here are some things that say to me, and I'm sure to you, that the Church of Jesus Christ of Latter-day Saints is the Kingdom of God on earth and that the Lord does honor those who serve Him. Those who fail to recognize the blessings that come with real service miss out on so much.

Now let me tell you just a few more personal experiences that happened to me.

All the experiences that I've told you before have happened within this mission during the time I've been in Idaho. Let me tell you just a few more experiences that I've had the privilege of being a part of since I've been a member of the Church. Most of you probably know that I'm a convert to the Church. I've been in the Church for ten years. Some of you may have read my conversion story. It's in Volume 2 of Hartman Rector's book, *No More Strangers*. Shortly after I joined the Church, I attended a church meeting in which there was a family in attendance with a small child. Nothing particularly unusual about that except for the circumstances that occurred a few days previous to that church meeting.

The child, who was about one year old, was playing outside in the driveway. The father was in a hurry to go to work. The father rushed to his car, not noticing the child in the driveway. The father backed his car down the driveway and felt a thud. He got out and looked at his child—limp, lifeless, with tire tracks right over the front part of the forehead. The father didn't know what to do. Then he thought, "Why would that happen to me?"

He thought about some of the things that representatives of the Lord were able to do, and he said to himself, "Why not me?"

He picked up that child in his arms, rushed her to the hospital, and called another member of the branch. They held that lifeless child in their arms. I won't say she was dead. I don't know whether she was dead or not. All I know is that the car had backed over her, and the tire tracks were right over her head. The child wasn't stirring.

They gave a blessing to that child and said, "By the power of the priesthood which we hold, and in the name of Jesus Christ, be made whole."

Now, I saw that child that Sunday, laughing, playing, just as alive as any of you are today. I watched that child grow up. The child is healthy. The child is making excellent grades in school now. Nothing wrong with her brain. A beautiful young girl. No one, after observing that kind of experience, could say to me that the Church isn't true. No one could convince me in any way that we are not members of a church where the Lord blesses us and honors those that live righteously enough to demonstrate the power of the Lord in the things that they do.

(Note: This child's name was Gay Golden. She is married, lives in Kennesaw, Georgia, and now goes by her married name of Galena Cattel. The father is Jim Golden and now lives in Tifton, Georgia. He and his wife are members of the Tifton Georgia Stake. The other member assisting in the blessing was Glen Singleton, who was branch president of the Albany, Georgia Branch at the time. Glen died a few years ago. Many of the names of individuals with similar experiences are not given due to the sacred nature of the experiences. Jim gave me permission to include his name in this book, however, and that is why I include it now.)

You know, six or seven or eight thousand years ago, or even further back, there was a council in Heaven, and the Plan of Salvation was presented there. In this council in Heaven, and we were all there, a plan was presented where we could go back and live with our Heavenly Father after coming to this earth and gaining a body so that we could become more like our Heavenly Father. We all had the opportunity to say whether or not we wanted to be a part of this great blessing, and we all said yes.

That's why we're here—because before we came to this earth, we made commitments. As we heard the commandments, we agreed that we would accept and follow those things that we had been taught in our preexistence.

We said we'd do it, and even then, some of us recognized our weaknesses and were concerned because we knew that we could not go back and live in the presence of our Heavenly Father if we were unclean. We knew that we were weak and probably wouldn't be able to keep all of the Commandments.

But there was one among us that could. It was Christ. And God said to Jesus Christ, "You can, if you'd like, go down, and you can be the Savior for the rest of your brothers and sisters. If you love them enough, if you are committed enough, you can go down, and as these others don't qualify because of the mistakes they will make, you can go down and be their Savior. Now, here's what it will take. People will abuse you and they'll curse you and they'll spit upon you. All those people that you're going to bless will put you to death. They won't put you to death in just a normal way. You won't be killed instantly. It will be slow death. In fact, they will see to it that you die the most agonizing type of death that is known to man. You'll have to go to a garden and pray, and there take upon yourself all the sins of the world. You'll suffer anguish so great that you will bleed at every pore. If you are willing to go down there, and if you'll still love these people that are doing that to you—if you're still committed that much—then the rest of the world—the rest of your brothers and sisters who are yet to come to earth—will have the privilege of coming back and living with their Heavenly Father—provided they're willing to accept your atonement and to repent and to be baptized and to endure to the end."

Christ said he would—and he did. To me, that was one of the best examples of commitment that has ever come forth. Now, you're called to commit your lives to the Savior, throughout this life and throughout eternity. You're called to share the things that you have with others. We're told in the scriptures (Doctrine and Covenants, Section 15, Verse 6) that the thing of most worth to us is to declare repentance unto this people, "that you may bring souls unto me. That you may rest with them in the Kingdom of my Father."

You are called to commit your life to service for one who committed His life to your service. You can answer that call by saying, "Why me?" or you can answer it by saying, "Why not me?" I trust you know the proper answer, and you will commit your lives to following the Savior.

I testify to you that the Church of Jesus Christ of Latter-day Saints is the Kingdom of God on earth. It's true. I testify to you that God lives and Jesus is the Christ, and you can speak to Him and He'll speak to you. As you dedicate your life to the service to the Master, the Lord will honor your prayers.

I testify to you that Joseph Smith was a prophet of God, and that Spencer W. Kimball is a prophet of God today. He gives us messages and instructions that will help our lives. I testify to you, that as you follow the Savior and the prophets, your life will be blessed now and throughout the eternities. That we might all, when we are called, cease to answer, "Why me?" and begin answering, "Why not me?" is my prayer in the Name of Jesus Christ, Amen.

Love,

Ritchey Marbury

"A single sunbeam is enough to drive away many shadows."

—SAINT FRANCIS OF ASSISI

Kansas City Temple

WILL

Dear Missionaries,

One of the greatest mistakes in life is giving up. Heavenly Father will never give up on us, so why should we give up on ourselves? Most of us remember Abraham Lincoln as one of the great presidents of the United States of America. I wonder where he would be, or even where this country would be if he had given up on many of his endeavors.

Abraham Lincoln failed in business in 1831. He was defeated for legislature in 1832. He failed again in business in 1833. He suffered a nervous breakdown in 1836. He was defeated for Congress in 1848. He was defeated for Senate in 1855. He was defeated for vice president in 1856. He was defeated again for Senate in 1858. Then in 1860 he was elected president of the United States.

You can do whatever you have the will to do which is right, and for which you have the determination to persist. You can learn much from this poem by Ella Wheeler Wilcox. It is simply titled "Will."

> There is no chance, no destiny, no fate,
> That can circumvent or hinder or control
> The firm resolve of a determined soul.
> Gifts count for nothing; will alone is great;
> All things give way before it, soon or late.

What obstacle can stay the mighty force
Of the sea-seeking river in its course,
Or cause the ascending orb of day to wait?
Each well-born soul must win what it deserves.
Let the fool prate of luck. The fortunate
Is he whose earnest purpose never swerves,
Whose slightest action or inaction serves
The one great aim. Why, even Death stands still,
And waits an hour sometimes for such a will.

Love,

Ritchey Marbury

"There is no chance, no destiny, no fate,
That can circumvent or hinder or control
The firm resolve of a determined soul."

—Ella Wheeler Wilcox

WISDOM FROM PROPHETS

Dear Missionaries,

"Surely the Lord God will do nothing, but He revealeth His secret unto His servants the prophets" (Amos 3:7). Eight prophets have guided the Church of Jesus Christ of Latter-day Saints since Fonda and I joined in 1969. We learned from each of them, and each stands out as having taught truths that enriched our lives.

David O. McKay was prophet when we first joined. He had already reintroduced the concept of Family Home Evening in 1964. It was a teaching that helped our family grow even closer during our children's formative years. He taught that no success can compensate for failure in the home and also the importance of every member a missionary.

Joseph Fielding Smith served as prophet from 1970 to 1972. His father first introduced the principle of Family Home Evening in 1915. Joseph Fielding Smith encouraged all members to practice this principle on Monday nights. He taught that all of us are only instruments in the Lord's hands, and reminded us that wickedness never was happiness.

Harold B. Lee was a major force in establishing the welfare system of the Church. He taught that what you give to others means more than any sermons we preach. He told us that there are times when your heart tells you things that your mind doesn't know. He said to be slow to condemn and quick to forgive. Fonda and I will always have a special place in our hearts for Harold B. Lee, for he was the one who sealed us together in the temple as husband and wife for time and all eternity.

Spencer W. Kimball was the prophet who announced the revelation instructing the Church to give the priesthood to every worthy male. He told us to lengthen our strides, quicken our pace, go forward by leaps and bounds.

Ezra Taft Benson reminded of the importance of the Book of Mormon. It is the keystone of our religion; it was written specifically for our day, and one will get closer to God by abiding by its precepts than by any other book. His sermon on pride was perhaps his most remembered sermon. He taught that pride was one of the greatest vices of our time. Beware of pride.

Howard W. Hunter was born in Boise, Idaho. He served as prophet only a short time but set an example of love and dedication all of his life. He taught that there is a God in Heaven who loves and cares about you and me.

Gordon B. Hinckley gave us the timely council to get out of debt. He warned of the dangers of debt just a few years before the great recession. Once in a meeting with President Hinckley, I heard him teach the importance of handbooks. We should know what is in them and follow them. However, he explained, following the inspiration from the Lord is even more important.

He taught all of us that we must know what the Lord wants us to do, and then do it. Follow the promptings of the Lord. When the family proclamation was issued on September 23, 1995, he told us all to strengthen our families, that the family is the fundamental unit of our society.

Thomas S. Monson is our prophet today, as I write these letters. His motto seems to be "To the Rescue." He teaches us that love is the very essence of the gospel; that Christ taught us to love God and love our neighbors; that blame keeps wounds open and only forgiveness heals. He teaches us to resolve to do a little better than we have done in the past, and that we should be kind and loving to those who do not share our beliefs and standards.

Wisdom From Prophets

The words of prophets teach us how to prepare for this life and our eternal life to come. May we pay more attention to their teachings—and follow them.

Love,

Ritchey Marbury

"Surely the Lord God will do nothing, but He revealeth His secret unto His servants the prophets."

—Amos 3:7

Joseph and Hyrum Smith Look Back at Nauvoo Temple

Wishbone or Backbone

Dear Missionaries,

William Becker said, "The individual activity of one man with backbone will do more than a thousand men with a mere wishbone." You can wait for circumstances to change, or you can begin now to change circumstances. You can be up one day and down another, depending on circumstances, or you can be up on good days and work to improve circumstances on the other days.

Winston Churchill showed backbone when he told the people of England to never give up. He said that "continuous effort—not strength or intelligence—is the key to unlocking our potential." His backbone led England to overcome Hitler's armies and invasions when success seemed impossible.

Joseph F. Smith taught, "After we have done all we could do for the cause of truth, and withstood the evil that men have brought upon us, and we have been overwhelmed by their wrongs, it is still our duty to stand. We cannot give up. We must not lie down. Great causes are not won in a single generation. To stand firm in the face of overwhelming opposition, when you have done all you can, is the courage of faith."

The Lord wants valiant men and women to build up His kingdom. His kingdom is not a place for a sponge or parasite, but a place of useful activity where all progress through mutual activity. You have no need to cease good works because you listen to those overcome by jealously. Wishbones serve us well only as they grow into backbones. Heirs to celestial exaltation will be anxiously engaged in good works regardless of circumstances.

The Lord said in Doctrine and Covenants 58:27, "Verily I say, men should be anxiously engaged in a good cause, and do many things of their own free will, and bring to pass much righteousness." As your wishbone grows into a backbone, the impossible becomes possible, and your backbone becomes an instrument of higher law and divine purpose.

Love,

Ritchey Marbury

"The individual activity of one man with backbone will do more than a thousand men with a mere wishbone."

—William Becker

Words Of Wisdom From The Past

Dear Missionaries,

Sometimes it is fun to read messages from the past. In May 1974 I wrote a short article for the *Albany Branch News*, a newsletter prepared monthly by the Albany, Georgia, branch of the Church. It is a ward today, but those times as a branch were fun and rewarding. Here is part of what I wrote. Most of the ideas were not new then and are not new today. Still, I believe they are worth remembering.

Happiness is not a reward, but a consequence of righteous, positive action. It is our privilege to dedicate our talent, money, and time to the service of our Heavenly Father. To those whom much is given, much is expected. We can all do ordinary things in extraordinary ways. Our reward will be in direct proportion to our contribution.

We are what we repeatedly do. Excellence is not an act, but a habit. Do not procrastinate good works. What the foolish man does in the end, the wise man does in the beginning. A little thing is a little thing, but doing little things well is a big thing. As we acquire the habit of excellence now, we will more fully realize our effectiveness in the future. Why wait to do big things later when we can do a little good every day. Those busy doing the Lord's work have little time to argue over His plans. Do right and leave the results to God.

Love,

Ritchey Marbury

"Why wait to do big things later when we can do a little good every day."

—Ritchey Marbury

The Angel Moroni

WORDS WITHOUT KNOWLEDGE

Dear Missionaries,

"Who is this that darkeneth counsel by words without knowledge?" (Job 38:2).

These words from the Lord to Job are as applicable today as in Biblical times. Our wisdom is nothing compared to that of our Heavenly Father. Sometimes we think we are wise because we can build dams, erect skyscrapers, and harness electricity. We can make fashionable clothes and navigate from anywhere. Are we really so smart?

Heavenly Father created all things and gave nature abilities long before the birth of any of us. The human race is proud of its ability to build dams and construct skyscrapers. Beavers, however, constructed dams from the beginning of history. Colonies of termites build skyscraper termitaria twenty feet high and two hundred yards long that are impervious to water and maintain a constant temperature.

Before we harnessed electricity, the electric ray could generate 220 volts through its body at will. The firefly still gives engineers a goal worth matching. It can produce light virtually without heat. Our tailors could take lessons from the Indian tailorbird. It builds its nest between leaves sewn together with grass fibers.

Do we think we are the best navigators that ever lived? We still do not understand the ability of the homing pigeon to find its way home over long distances. When we tend to doubt the truthfulness of one of the Lord's directives, let us ask ourselves, "Are we yet all knowing?"

Just because we say something isn't so doesn't make it false. Heavenly Father teaches us truths through the scriptures, living prophets, and prayer. Failure to comprehend a truth makes it no less valid.

Love,

Ritchey Marbury

"Some never learn anything, because they know everything too soon."

—Author Unknown

IDEAS FOR MISSIONARY SERVICE

Dear Missionaries,

Missionary service is fun. Here are several ways to give service as a missionary. Use them yourselves and encourage your stake, ward, and branch leaders to use them, also.

HOME EVENING WITH FRIENDS NIGHT. Have a special "Home Evening with Friends" night. A stake, ward, or branch could demonstrate a Family Home Evening approach particularly suited for our nonmember friends. A family could plan such an event themselves. The family invites friends to their home for this special evening. The lesson should be short, leaving time for questions and fun activities together.

HOME EVENING DEMONSTRATION. Arrange with local civic clubs to demonstrate a Family Home Evening. Civic clubs are anxious for good programs. Plan an interesting and entertaining program. Discuss the program with the civic club leaders and stress how it helps families grow closer. This is not the time to proselyte. It is a time to show how our church teaches Christ-centered principles that bind families together.

ANNUAL NEW CONVERT DINNER. Have an annual dinner honoring new converts. Have the new converts invite nonmember friends to the dinner. Do not charge for this activity. Plan fun entertainment followed by a short inspirational talk from one or two converts. Invite the speakers in advance and do not turn this into a testimony meeting, which is not always enjoyable to nonmembers. Keep the talks short and focus on fun activities. Such a dinner helps new converts feel loved and provides a good social event that brings nonmembers, new converts, and members closer together.

AARONIC PRIESTHOOD APPOINTMENTS. *"Therefore, take with you those who are ordained unto the lesser priesthood, and send them before you to make appointments, and to prepare the way, and to fill appointments that you yourselves are not able to fill"* (Doctrine and Covenants 84:107). Youth ages fourteen through eighteen could devote three hours one afternoon, perhaps on a Sunday, going through safe neighborhoods visiting homes accompanied by an adult advisor. They should dress appropriately. They could knock on doors and ask those at the door if they would allow missionaries to visit them on a particular evening, to share a special message about Christ. The youth then give these appointments to the full-time missionaries. On the arranged night, if desired, the youth could go with the full-time missionaries to the appointments.

NEIGHBORHOOD PARTIES. *"A friend loveth at all times"* (Proverbs 17:17). Be a friend to gain a friend. Invite the neighborhood together for an afternoon or evening of fun and refreshments, perhaps every six months. During the winter this could be a neighborhood outing, a snowmobile or sledding trip (if you live where it snows), a sing-along, a marshmallow or wiener roast, an open house, etc. A picnic would be fun during the warmer season, or a fish fry. The purpose is not to teach the gospel at this time, but to have fun together as friends. Later, after prayer, invite a few of these friends to visit in your home for the missionaries to teach. First, however, just love your neighbors, make friends, and have fun together.

MISSIONARY COMMITTEE CHAIRPERSON. Invite every church auxiliary and quorum to call a missionary committee chairperson. Have missionary service on every meeting agenda. Missionary chairpersons keep auxiliaries and quorums reminded of missionary opportunities and serve as a resource for missionary service. They can also show ways missionary service will increase the success of other church organizations and programs.

FAMILY MISSIONARY COMMITTEE. Families form a family organization and call one member of the family to chair a Family Missionary Committee. Two or three other family members could be a part of the committee. The purpose is to organize and implement missionary activity within the family. Activities could include inviting nonmembers or less active members into their home for missionary discussions, or personalizing copies of the Book of Mormon for use by the full-time missionaries.

BOOK OF MORMON PLACEMENT. Place family photographs in copies of the Book of Mormon with your testimony on the same page as the photographs. Give to friends or to the full-time missionaries.

SELECT, FRIENDSHIP, INVITE. Prayerfully select a family or families to friendship. Have friendshipping activities together. Invite them into your home to be taught by the full-time missionaries.

MISSIONARY SETTLEMENT. Priesthood leaders hold a "missionary settlement" with each family. It could follow the format of a tithing settlement, where the family reports on their missionary efforts and experiences. This should not be a "scolding session" for what was not done, but an opportunity to express gratitude for service rendered and to offer motivation for future service.

COMPLETE YOUR ETERNAL FAMILY MONTH. Invite all unbaptized members over the age of eight to hear the missionary discussions, and prepare for baptism, completing the first step for an eternal family unit. Preparation for temple sealing could follow.

DO YOU LIKE TO READ? Have a "Do You Like to Read?" month. Encourage a member of every family to ask a nonmember friend, or even a stranger, two questions: (1) Do you like to read? Regardless of the answer, then ask, (2) If I send you a book containing the actual account of the visit of Jesus Christ to America, will you read it? Most will answer, "Yes." Then ask them to write their name, address, and phone number on your business card or some other piece of paper. Give the card to the missionaries with a personalized copy of the Book of Mormon. The missionaries then deliver it.

SET A DATE. Set a specific date to have another family or friend taught the gospel in your home. Tell the full-time missionaries of the date and pray to know whom the Lord would have you invite.

About The Author

Ritchey Marbury joined the Church of Jesus Christ of Latter-day Saints with his wife, Fonda, on September 4, 1969. Charlie Sellers, Ritchey's college classmate, gave Ritchey a copy of the Book of Mormon in 1961. They were both graduate students at Georgia Tech studying city planning. Ritchey read the book in two days, studied the Church for eight years, and was baptized with his wife. Their conversion story is found in Volume 2 of Hartman and Connie Rector's book *No More Strangers*.

Since joining, their love of Jesus Christ and the Church has grown stronger every day. Ritchey has served as branch president, bishop, stake president, mission president, and other callings. Fonda has served as mission president's companion, counselor in young women's presidency, ward organist, pianist in both primary and relief society, and other responsibilities. Ritchey says his favorite calling was den dad while his son was a cub scout and his wife was den mother.

Ritchey currently serves as the ward high priest group leader and also as a Church Service Missionary Photographer. Fonda serves as ward organist and also with Ritchey as a Church Service Missionary, primarily tagging photographs.

In 1949, at the age of eleven, Ritchey began his professional career as a land surveyor and civil engineer, working on a survey crew with his dad. After serving two years with the US Army Corps of Engineers, he returned home to obtain professional registrations as a land surveyor in 1965 and as a professional engineer in 1966. At age seventy-eight, he still works full time in these professions and plans to slow down to a forty-hour work week at age one hundred. He and Fonda plan never to slow down, however, in serving Jesus Christ and His church.

www.ingramcontent.com/pod-product-compliance
Lightning Source LLC
Chambersburg PA
CBHW061427040426
42450CB00007B/928